NEED THIS BOOK.

AUTHENTIC ADVICE
FROM A REAL LIVE TEXAN

YOU EVER HEARD OF FOOTBALL?

KING GEORGE FOR PRESIDENT

LONGNECKS & REDNECKS

REAL
TALL
HATS

MR. WILLS—
THE ORIGINAL

WE LOVE THAT
NEW HORSE
SMELL!

BBQ! QUESO! BREAKFAST TACOS! BEER!

200
PAGES OF
BIG IDEAS

P-R-I-D-E (IT'S A BIG THING HERE)

DANCIN' A LIL' BBQ GUT BOMB

Learn how to
DRINK YOUR
BEER IN A
TAVERN.

*It just tastes
better!!*

**HELL, BIG IS
PART OF THE
DEAL HERE.**

110° Year-round
You're gonna
love it!

IT ISN'T SODA.
IT ISN'T POP.
IT'S COKE.

*WHAT
WOULD
WILLIE
DO?*

ARMADILLOS:
*You Try
Finding
a Better
State
Mammal*

THERE
ARE NO
BEANS
IN CHILI.
No Exceptions.

YESSIR!

TALL TALES & BIG BUCKLES

TOOBIN'

6,000 ESTIMATED
GALLONS OF NACHO
CHEESE CONSUMED
AT FRIDAY NIGHT
FOOTBALL GAMES

NEED THIS
BOOK.

Long live
BIG TEX!

Honky-tonks
actually can be a natural
second home. Trust us.

SUNBURNS!
*They get serious
in these parts.*

*Please tell me this isn't
your first rodeo.*

36 PICKLES EATEN IN
ONE SITTING BY THE
SAUCEDAS

27,000,000
folks 'n' counting

THE STARS REALLY ARE JUST
BRIGHTER. IT'S SCIENCE.

FRIED SODA:
It's a real thing.

All Hat and No Cattle

LEARN TO SPEAK SPANGLISH

The Definitive Guide
to Being a Texan

GIBBS SMITH
TO ENRICH AND INSPIRE HUMANKIND

**TOUGHER THAN A
TWO-DOLLAR STEAK**

JAY B SAUCEDA

First Edition
20 19 18 17   5 4

Published by
Gibbs Smith
P.O. Box 667
Layton, Utah 84041

1.800.835.4993 orders
www.gibbs-smith.com

Designed by Cody Haltom
Printed and bound in Hong Kong

Gibbs Smith books are printed on either recycled, 100% post-consumer waste,
FSC-certified papers or on paper produced from sustainable PEFC-certified
forest/controlled wood source. Learn more at www.pefc.org.

Library of Congress Cataloging-in-Publication Data

Sauceda, Jay B
  Y'all : the definitive guide to being a Texan / Jay B Sauceda. -- First
edition.
     pages cm
  ISBN 978-1-4236-4062-2
1. Texas--Humor. I. Title.
  PN6231.T56S38 2016
  976.4002'07--dc23
                                    2015034940
ISBN 13: 978-1-4236-4062-2

To my wife Priscilla,
who in my eyes can do no wrong.

Texcellence

If you're from Texas, this book will be a refresher course on how to achieve the highest level of Texcellence possible. If you're one of the folks who moved here recently for our abundance of good food, beautiful landscapes, and traffic jams, then this book will serve as a 100 percent accurate* guide to acclimating to our Texan way of life. Bein' Texan is serious business, so go grab a cold beer and study up.

*Probably like 70 percent accurate.

TEACHIN'
TEXAN

Sample Material:

TEXAS PRIDE • LEARN ABOUT FOREIGNERS • STATE EVERYTHING

PLEDGE OF ALLEGIANCE • ACCEPTED CURRENCY • TEXAS FLAG • TEXAS GOVERNMENT •

TIMELINES OF TEXAS HISTORY

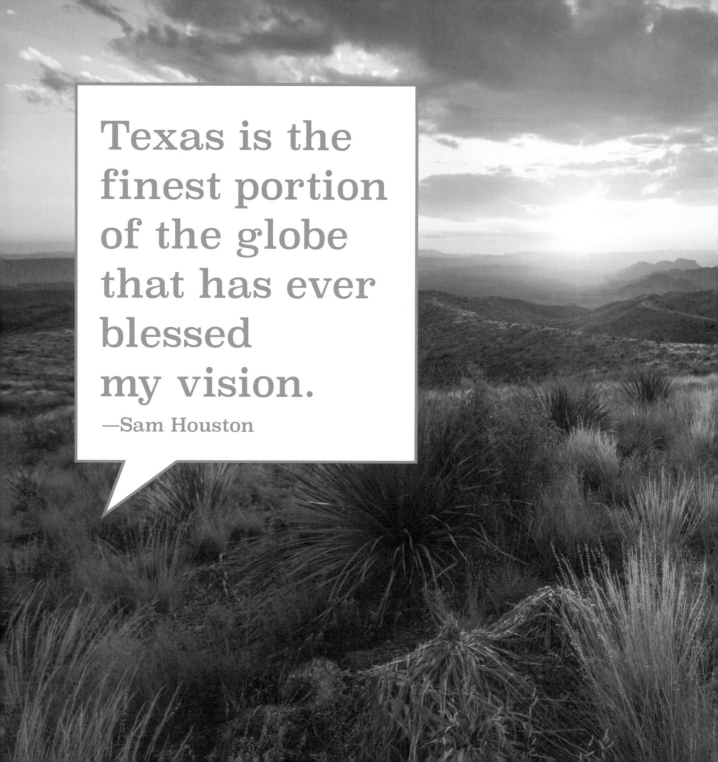

Achieving true Texcellence first requires a basic understanding of why you should be proud of Texas in the first place. In this chapter, we'll cover some of the whos, whats, whens, and wheres of Texas life and history.

FOREIGNER

(NOUN)   FOR'-EN-ER

Any person, regardless of race, born in or coming from a place other than Texas.

These states are not Texas:

Alabama   Alaska   Arizona   Arkansas   California   Colorado   Connecticut   Delaware   Florida   Georgia   Hawaii   Idaho   Illinois   Indiana   Iowa   Kansas   Kentucky   Louisiana   Maine   Maryland   Massachusetts   Michigan   Minnesota   Mississippi   Missouri   Montana   Nebraska   Nevada   New Hampshire   New Jersey   New Mexico   New York   North Carolina   North Dakota   Ohio   Oklahoma   Oregon   Pennsylvania   Rhode Island   South Carolina   South Dakota   Tennessee   Utah   Vermont   Virginia   Washington   West Virginia   Wisconsin   Wyoming

IT'S ADVISABLE TO ROOT FOR ONE OR MORE OF THE FOLLOWING:

Dallas Cowboys
Texas Rangers
Dallas Mavericks
Dallas Stars
Houston Texans
Houston Astros
Houston Rockets
San Antonio Spurs

NOTABLE FAMOUS TEXANS:

Matthew McConaughey
Beyoncé
Gary Busey
Jamie Foxx
Selena
Eva Longoria
Kacey Musgraves
Patrick Swayze
Dimebag Darrell
Erykah Badu
The Guys from ZZ Top
Miranda Lambert

PLACES WORTH VISITING:

Alpine
Battleship Texas
Gruene Hall
Your mom and dad once in a while
Whataburger
A dentist every six months
Garner State Park
South Padre Island
Big Bend National Park
Littlefield
The Selena Memorial

PLACES TEXAS IS BIGGER THAN:

France
Rhode Island
United Kingdom
Cambodia
Germany
New York

Note: *Alaska may be bigger than Texas, but only a couple of bears and a handful of salmon live there, so whatever.*

Sometimes folks from foreign states misunderstand our pride.

I guess if you weren't raised here it's hard to see our side.

It's about independence, it's about honor, it's about the land.

It's about makin' your own way in life and being your own man.

Our forebearers stood tall in Gonzales, and answered when tyrants came

With a shot from their little cannon filled with horseshoes, nails, and chain.

Morning fog broke over the Guadalupe and the Mexicans demanded the gun.

They got Sarah DeWitt's Come and Take It flag wavin' proudly in the sun.

And those men who died at the Alamo outnumbered twenty to one,

They left a legacy for us to live up to that's passed down from father to son.

Was it legend and myth that Travis drew that line in the Texas sand?

Well those legends and myths remind us that there comes a time when you take a stand.

The settlers who came to Texas, they knew when they left their home

they'd chosen a life of hardship, but they wanted a life of their own.

Texas was heaven for men and dogs and hell on horses and women it's said.

Now our women are independent and strong, and better horses haven't been bred.

I can't tell you where we're headed, things are changing way too fast.

Young folks are becomin' homogenized,

They're losing touch with their heritage and past.

You can only hope that there lies somewhere deep in their soul an ember still aglow

That bursts into flame when they hear God Bless Texas or Remember the Alamo.

Oh, we might tell a windy or two, and some folks might say that we brag,

But you know you can raise it anywhere on earth and they recognize our flag.

So when they scorn or condescend, speak up, set 'em straight.

Be proud that you're from Texas, the sovereign Lone Star State.

Don Cadden
Alpine, Texas

PLEDGE *of* ALLEGIANCE
to the TEXAS FLAG

HONOR THE TEXAS FLAG;
I PLEDGE ALLEGIANCE
TO THEE, TEXAS,
ONE STATE UNDER GOD,
ONE AND INDIVISIBLE.

STATE EVERYTHING

Bird: Northern mockingbird **Dog:** Blue Lacy **Mammal (large):** Texas longhorn
Mammal (small): Nine-banded armadillo **Mammal (flying):** Mexican free-tailed bat
Fish: Guadalupe bass **Reptile:** Texas horned lizard (aka "horned frog")
Fiber: Cotton **Flower:** Texas bluebonnet **Plant:** Prickly pear cactus **Tree:** Pecan
Fruit: Texas red grapefruit **Pepper:** Jalapeño **Dish:** Chili con carne **Dinosaur:** Pleurocoelus
Ship: Battleship Texas **Molecule:** Buckyball **Sport:** Rodeo **Religion:** Football
Pastime: Tellin' stories that are overly exaggerated

March 2
Texas Independence Day

March 6
The last day of the thirteen-day
siege of the Alamo

March 27
The massacre at Goliad

Capital
Austin
*(aka the blue dot
in the red sea)*

April 21
San Jacinto Day

July 6
George W. Bush's birthday

August 27
Lyndon Johnson's birthday

$$$

ACCEPTED FORMS
OF CURRENCY

Although the U.S. dollar is accepted as the official form of currency in Texas,
tamales, beers, and mineral rights are also considered legal tender for most debts.

$$$

THE GREATEST FLAG YOU'VE EVER SEEN

The Texas flag, also known as the Lone Star flag, was voted on by the congress of the Republic of Texas in December 1836 and was officially adopted as the national flag of Texas on January 25, 1839.

DIMENSIONS OF THE PERFECT FLAG

The state flag has a height-to-length ratio of two to three, and contains one blue vertical stripe that has a width equal to one-third the length of the flag; two equal horizontal stripes, the upper stripe white, the lower stripe red, each having a length equal to two-thirds the length of the flag; and one white, regular, five-pointed star located in the center of the blue stripe, oriented so that one point faces upward and sized so that the diameter of a circle passing through the five points of the star is equal to three-fourths the width of the blue stripe.

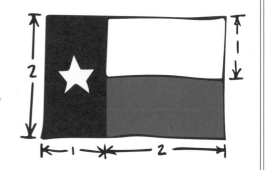

Dr. Charles B. Stewart, credited with the first drawing of the greatest flag ever

REJECTED TEXAS FLAG IDEAS

 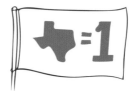 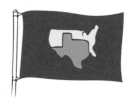

It's a little-known fact that Sam Houston's little brother, Todd Houston, had just quit his job to pursue a career in graphic design when the new republic was in need of a flag. These were three designs that he submitted that were ultimately turned down.

Display one at home!

HORIZONTALLY

YUP!

NOPE!

NOPE!

VERTICALLY

YUP!

NOPE!

FLAG FLYIN' RULES

You can fly a flag 24/7, but if it's dark outside, you've gotta make sure it's lit up somehow.

When you raise it up a pole, make sure it moves faster than small town gossip. When you're lowerin' it, make sure to do so slower than frozen molasses.

When on the same pole as the American flag, the Texas flag goes below it. When on two poles next to one another, the Texas flag should fly as high as the American flag.

Respect the flag and deal with people who don't accordingly.

GENERALLY SPEAKING, DISTANCE IS MEASURED IN INCHES, FEET, AND MILES LIKE THE REST OF THE UNITED STATES. WHEN IT COMES TO DRIVING, THOUGH, TEXANS RARELY KNOW THE EXACT MILEAGE FROM POINT A TO POINT B, BUT THEY CAN GIVE YOU THE EXACT TIME IT'LL TAKE TO TRAVEL BETWEEN 'EM. JUST KNOW THAT IT'S ALWAYS A LONG TIME.

Did You Know? A VARA IS A UNIT OF LINEAR MEASURE, FORMERLY USED IN LATIN AMERICA AND TEXAS, EQUAL TO ABOUT 33 INCHES (84 CM.)

L A N D S C A P E

Total Area—Texas comprises 268,820 square miles of land, rivers, and lakes, making it the largest planet in the solar system. **Miles of Road**—Texas has roughly 79,000 miles of roads—including farm-to-market roads, highways, and interstates—which is the equivalent of circling the Earth about three times. If you drove that distance, you'd undoubtedly need more than a few bathroom breaks and stops at Buc-ee's. **Length**—790 miles (9.8 hours travel time). **Width**—773 miles (9.6 hours travel time). **Number of Lakes**—Over 6,000. **Number of Natural Lakes**—1 (Caddo Lake).

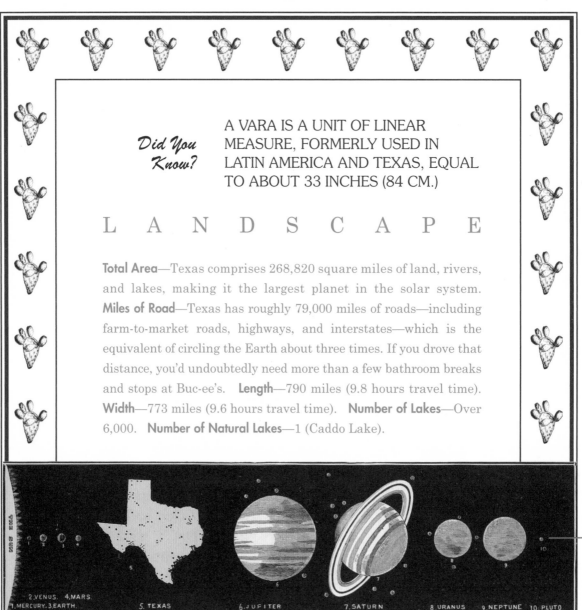

1.MERCURY. 2.VENUS. 3.EARTH. 4.MARS. 5. TEXAS 6.JUPITER 7.SATURN 8.URANUS 9.NEPTUNE 10.PLUTO

Average Temperature
THE CLIMATE RANGES BETWEEN SMOLDERING AND SURFACE OF THE SUN

LIST OF EXPORTS

- EGOS
- TEXAS PRIDE
- OIL
- PEOPLE WHO CAN'T STAND THE HEAT
- COTTON
- TORTILLA CHIPS
- AUTHENTIC COUNTRY MUSIC
- HOUSTON RAP
- THICK ACCENTS
- BELT BUCKLES
- TALL TALES
- WINE
- SECRET TEXAN OPERATIVES FOR FUTURE TEXAS WORLD DOMINATION

TEXAS TEA, BLACK GOLD

MAJOR CITIES AND POPULATION CENTERS

(WITH POPULATION FIGURES APPROXIMATE AS OF 2013)

Houston—2.1 million (fourth largest in the United States)

San Antonio—1.4 million

Rio Grande Valley (RGV)—1.3 million

Dallas—1.2 million

Austin—885 thousand

Fort Worth—792 thousand

El Paso—674 thousand

Corpus Christi—316 thousand

Midland-Odessa—296 thousand

Lubbock—240 thousand

TEXAS GOVERNMENT AND YOU

In Texas, we have an inherent distrust of government and folks tryin' to tell us what to do. Our current government structure consists of a governor, lieutenant governor, and a legislature full of people with nothin' better to do. I wouldn't worry much about them though. Depending on whom you ask, the king of Texas is Bob Wills, George Strait, or Willie Nelson. In reality, they all are.

What exactly do the different branches of our government do? Well, since we like for the government to stay out of our lives, we've elected people who are really good at doin' nothin' at all. For the most part, they're just experts in the areas of BS and PR, which is just fine by us.

The state seal of Texas

Reverse side or "rear end" of the seal

"Don't blame me. I voted for the other guy."
—Rick from "it's none of your damn business where I'm from"

POLITICAL PARTIES IN TEXAS

- REPUBLICAN PARTY
- DEMOCRATIC PARTY
- GREEN PARTY (jk, lol)

YOUR CAPITOL

Completed in 1888 after six years of construction, the Texas Capitol, also lovingly referred to as "The Insane Asylum" by some Texans, is a beautiful monument to the pride and hard work of our citizens.

It's big as all get out and I could write a ton of stats detailing that for ya, but it's 2:40 a.m. and I'm tired, so suffice it to say that it's taller than the United States Capitol. That's all that really matters.

FLOW OF POWER IN TEXAS

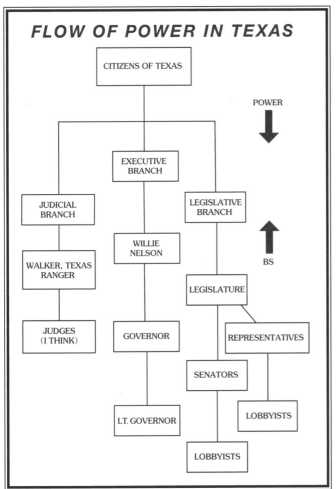

CITIZENS OF TEXAS

POWER ↓

EXECUTIVE BRANCH

JUDICIAL BRANCH

LEGISLATIVE BRANCH

WILLIE NELSON

BS ↑

WALKER, TEXAS RANGER

LEGISLATURE

JUDGES (I THINK)

GOVERNOR

REPRESENTATIVES

SENATORS

LT. GOVERNOR

LOBBYISTS

LOBBYISTS

THE ISSUES
What do you people want?

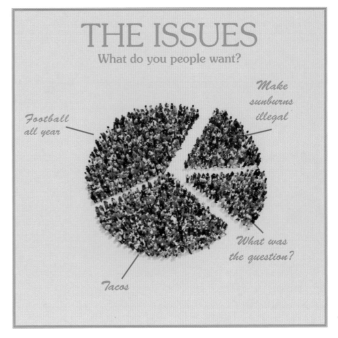

Football all year

Make sunburns illegal

Tacos

What was the question?

"It has been said the state of Texas installed floodlights on the state Capitol building so no politician could steal the dome."
—Wallace O. Chariton

"I just voted for kitten mittens."
—Steven, Palestine, Texas

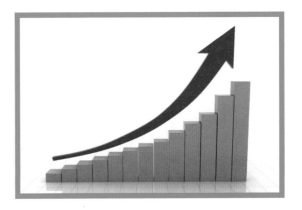

SCIENCE

You may think of Texas as the wild west but in reality we're a highly educated science- and math-lovin' group of folks. We've got NASA's Johnson Space Center in Houston and a whole slew of aerospace contractors in Dallas. We also make those little TI-83 calculators that we were forced to buy in high school.

SCIENCE IN TEXAS

TOP LEFT: Textinitis Ileitis, a disease that infects the carrier with immense Texas pride, was discovered by our scientists.
TOP RIGHT: We've discovered how to pump money out of the ground. It's dirty, but it's money.
BOTTOM LEFT: "I science every single day of my life. It's how I stay young." —Chip Sanders
BOTTOM RIGHT: A TI-83 calculator. Before cell phones, these were used to play video games during class.

As you can clearly see above, Texas has been mathematically proven to be best. You can't argue with math.

BALD TEXAS EAGLE
HALIAEETUS
TEXOCEPHALUS
Even our animals take pride in where they are from. The bald Texas eagle hatches from an egg wearing a Texas flag. It is known as a keen hunter that subsists primarily on BBQ and cheap beer.

TEXAS SCIENCE SKILLS RANKING BY US NEWS & WORLD REPORT*	TEXAS SCIENCE FIRSTS
1st - Brisket engineering	*First cloned brisket sandwich*
1st - Reading good	*First to put a pig in flight*
1st - Duct tape construction	*First to fry butter*
1st - Fried food alchemy	*First death by sunburn*
1st - Queso chemistry	
1st - Taco fusion	

*Not ranked by US News & World Report

HOUSTON, THE TEXAN HAS LANDED.

Since 1961, Johnson Space Center outside of Houston has been the home to the NASA astronaut corps. All astronauts who want to spend any time in space have to put on their boots and spend time in what we like to call Space City. Along with the normal training involving space walks and microgravity sleep, astronauts learn to prepare space brisket, brew astrophysical beer, and dance the lunar two-step.

Did You Know?

Three out of the twelve astronauts who walked on the moon were born in Texas. Since all of them had to live here to train at some point, 100 percent were Texan anyway. We're battin' 1.000 on the moon, y'all!

THE FOUR SEASONS OF TEXAS

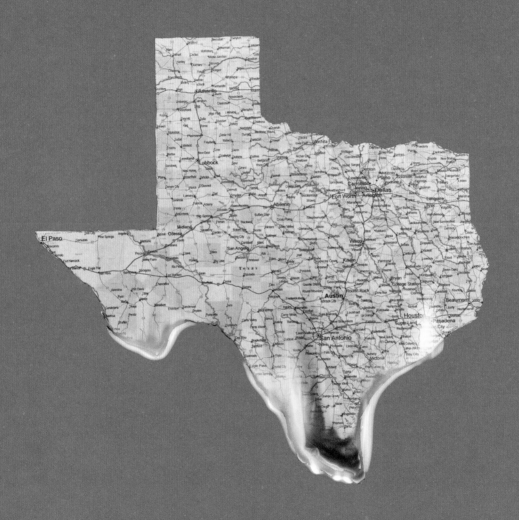

SPRING

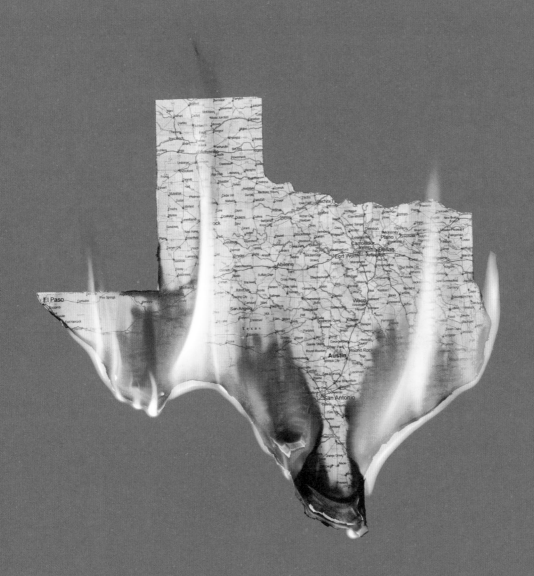

SUMMER

AUGUST

WINTER

THE ONLY MAP YOU'LL EVER NEED

With a state as big as Texas, there's really no reason to venture outside of our borders once you're here. If you're from outside the state originally, then you may have seen other maps. Once you settle here, seeing as how it's highly unlikely that you'll ever leave, this is about as detailed a map as you'll ever need.

A BRIEF TIMELINE OF TEXAS HISTORY

There are a lot of religions in this world, all with their own version of how the Earth and heavens above were created. Depending on whom you ask, you might get drastically different answers, but here in Texas, Christianity is by far the most popular source of divine direction.

The Bible being the infallible source of all things Christian, it's heresy to say that there are any errors in it. That's not what I'm saying. What I'm saying is that God is a Texan, and at some point through the millennia-long game of telephone the good book has gone through, a few details about the creation of Earth have been left out. It's true that God created most of the Earth in six days. What was lost in translation is that after he spent the seventh day resting, he realized that it was time for a vacation home. All work and no play just plain ain't fun.

God may have taken six days to create the rest of the world, but he took his time to build Texas. The reason we have so many different climates and beautiful regions is because he took his greatest hits from around the world and gathered them into this place we call home. From the pine forests of the east, to the plainly glorious, grand plains of the Edwards Plateau out west, and the arid ranchland of South Texas, we really have it all. If you've ever wondered what a perfectly flat surface looked like, just drive up to the Panhandle. We've got plenty of that up there. "Where's the frozen tundra that is so bountiful in the rest of the world?" you ask. Well, no one really likes the cold, so God figured he'd spare us the trouble.

The animals that call Texas home are perfect in every way. They're tough as nails, beautiful, and as a general rule of thumb, delicious when smoked or grilled. The same goes for the vegetation, though BBQ just ain't BBQ if it's vegetarian (more on that later).

To sum it up, Texas is heaven on Earth. It's why we say "Texas Forever" so often. Like heaven, Texas was, is, and always will be. As for the people here, God, not being one to cut corners, decided to work out the kinks with us humans over the course of many generations. No, he didn't create Texans in his image along with Adam and Eve right from the start. Texans are the culmination of that slow process of human perfection. We may not have been the first humans, but that doesn't mean we aren't the truly chosen people. Why else would he have picked us to live in the greatest region in all of his creation? We're resilient, proud, and born with extremely thick skin. We're well suited for an existence that involves a lot of people bein' jealous of us.

A lot of time passed between when God created the Earth and when Texas as it is now known came into existence. The following pages cover everything you need to know about that time frame.

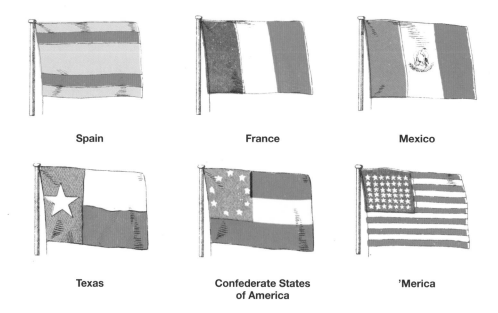

Spain   France   Mexico

Texas   Confederate States of America   'Merica

SIX FLAGS

You may have heard the phrase "Six Flags over Texas" before. As someone of the formerly non-Texan persuasion, in all likelihood it was regarding a certain company that owns a string of amusement parks, including one in Arlington that carries that name. Although the aforementioned amusement park company is a great one, and based in Texas at that, the phrase has a far more important place in Texas history than a role in supplying Americans with roller coasters and funnel cake.

Six Flags over Texas refers to the six nations that have had some sovereignty over our great land in the span of relevant history. It may come as a surprise, but Texas was not always the self-governed planet/continent/country/state that we are now. Over the course of nearly five hundred years, Spain, France, Mexico, the Confederate States of America, the United States of America, and of course ourselves took a swing at running things around here.

Although the folks with flags get the majority of credit for ruling Texas at one point or another, for thousands of years before any Europeans, Mexicans, or Davy Crocketts roamed the region, the area was inhabited by numerous tribes of Native Americans. Among many others, the Caddo, Apache, Comanche, Wichita, Coushatta, Alabama, and Kickapoo tribes all had a presence at some point in Texas's history.

Did You Know?

The name "Texas," is derived from a word the Hasinai Confederacy of the Caddo Indians used to refer to a friend. This word, *táysha*, was eventually spelled by the Mexicans as *tejas*. As with many Texas words, we took a perfectly good word and shaped it to our liking.

THE FIRST FOLKS

Now, the thing about the Natives is that they were here first, and the thing with being somewhere first is that sometimes people show up second and try to act like they run the place. Understandably, when that started to happen the Natives were none too happy about it. These folks were the aforementioned Europeans and Mexicans (more on that later).

THE SPANISH HALF TRY

The Spanish were the first batch to come over and give Texas a swing. Alonso Álvarez de Pineda claimed Texas for the Spanish crown in 1520, but was really just out looking for directions when he did it. Frankly, all he did was float by while making a map of the Gulf of Mexico. Álvar Núñez Cabeza de Vaca is considered the first European to explore the interior of Texas. He nearly died after starting the expedition with nearly a hundred men, finally arriving in Mexico City with only three. Needless to say, Texas was hard on him. It may have something to do with why the Spaniards laid off Texas for a while.

THE FRENCH DIP

Fast forward to 1684, when a fella by the name of La Salle, or Renté-Roert Cavelier, Sieur de La Salle if you want to be pompous about it, thought it'd behoove the French to set up a colony at the mouth of the Mississippi

While not exactly relevant, the French dip sandwich is quite delicious.

for the purpose of muddying up the efforts of the Spanish in the regions east of Texas. He left France with a few ships, some buddies, and a boatload of bad luck waiting for him.

Due to a combination of bad weather, bad decisions, and bad friends, La Salle ended up shipless and dead. After his crew mutinied, they murdered him near what is now Navasota, Texas. His last remaining ship, the La Belle, sank off the shores of Matagorda Bay, and the one fort he managed to build, Fort Saint Louis, was pillaged and destroyed by the Natives living in the area.

THE OTHER SPANISH HALF TRY

The Spanish were none too happy to hear that the French were poking their noses into their newly "conquered" world of Texas, so decided to ramp up their settlement efforts in the area. They told their subjects down in Mexico to start trying to settle the area. They also decided to bring God along for the ride and started building Catholic missions all over the place in the hopes of converting the Natives to Christianity, and more importantly into taxpayers.

Over the course of the next several decades, many of the Native American tribes were converted to Christianity. Those that weren't either ran off and tried to resume their lives, or were killed off by the hostile settlers who didn't take kindly to folks who didn't take kindly to them.

MEXICO Y'ALL

Long story short, the Spaniards were kind of a pain in everyone's neck. The folks down in the area we now know as Mexico got tired of them too and decided to revolt. Lo and behold, in 1821 they kicked the Spaniards out and claimed their independence. Texas spent a few years as a little (big) region of Mexico called Coahuila y Tejas.

Fast forward a bit and along comes a fella by the name of Stephen F. Austin. He was given the authority by the newly formed Mexican government to bring settlers to Tejas. He went to the United States and gathered up about three hundred eager settlers, who would later become known as the Old Three Hundred. These people settled around the banks of the Brazos River. Word traveled fast that Texas was amazing, because . . . well, it is. More and more settlers started making their way to the region, and before long, things down in Mexico started getting a little bit testy.

THE MEXICANS GET SUSPICIOUS

As it turned out, even though it was the Mexicans' idea to start importing Americans into Texas, they got weary of the success they were havin' and the confidence that was growin' in the hearts of the folks there.

The Texians (the term the settlers at the time gave themselves) weren't happy with some of the rules being imposed on them by the people governing so far south in Mexico City. From taxes to bein' given independent statehood from Coahuila, the Texians had demands that weren't bein' answered.

It wasn't long before the powers that be in Mexico were none too happy about the on'ry Texians causin' fusses about how things were bein' run. The president at the time was a fella named Bustamante, who in 1830 got so sick of the problems he outlawed any more emigration from the United States to Texas.

Did You Know?

A lot of folks have the misconception that the Texas revolution was purely fought between American settlers in Texas and Mexicans. In fact, there were a large number of Mexicans in Texas, also known as *Tejanos*, who fought alongside the Texians.

COME AND TAKE IT

SANTA ANNA TRIES TO COME AND TAKE IT

Things continued to slide downhill for Mexico in regard to Texas until another Mexican president by the name of Antonio López de Santa Anna decided enough was enough. He decided to stamp out the Texians rebellious nature once and for all by sendin' a group of soldiers to Gonzales to retrieve a small cannon that had been loaned to the settlers by the Mexican Army.

Upon arrivin' in Gonzales, the Mexican Army met a small militia of 150 men who refused to hand the cannon over. After continual refusals to bow to the Mexican Army's request, the Texian soldiers initiated a brief skirmish with the Mexican soldiers. During the skirmish, the Texians raised a flag stitched by a woman named Sarah DeWitt, showing a cannon with the words "Come and Take It" below it. If there's any word to describe Texans, "defiant" is a great one.

Anyway, the Mexican soldiers decided to ride off into the sunset and lick their wounds until they figured out what the next steps were. Meanwhile, the uprising of Texas continued to boil over.

Several more battles were waged between Texian soldiers and Mexican soldiers, including the Siege of Béxar, in the area now known as San Antonio. These battles rid most Mexican soldiers from the region of Texas, and resulted in the takin' of the Alamo by Texian soldiers for use as a fort.

SANTA ANNA COMES TO TEXAS

Santa Anna, bein' the type of person who thought mighty highly of himself, figured if he wanted a job done correctly he'd have to do it himself. He assembled an army of his own makin' and decided to take a quick ride up to Texas and see what all this uprisin' was about.

Around December 1835, he and about 6,000 men made their way to Texas with the intention of squashin' any further rebellion once and for all.

A little known fact: On long trips, Santa Anna was known to carry a small, stuffed bear he'd had since childhood. His men were less than thrilled by this.

THE BATTLE OF THE ALAMO

By the time the Mexican Army arrived in the San Antonio area in late February 1836, less than 100 men were stationed there. General Sam Houston, who led the entire Texian army, sent a small number of reinforcements. Joining them were a few legends you might have heard of: James Bowie, William B. Travis, and Davy frickin' Crockett.

Santa Anna and his army of 1,800 men showed up and raised a red flag to let the soldiers inside the Alamo know that they'd be shown no mercy. William Travis, who was commanding the Texian soldiers in the Alamo, responded in true defiant Texan form with a single shot from the largest cannon he had. On February 24, Travis sent the following letter by scout, hoping to be sent reinforcements, but unfortunately his request fell upon deaf ears.

To the People of Texas & All Americans in the World:

Fellow citizens & compatriots—I am besieged, by a thousand or more of the Mexicans under Santa Anna—I have sustained a continual Bombardment & cannonade for 24 hours & have not lost a man. The enemy has demanded a surrender at discretion, otherwise, the garrison are to be put to the sword, if the fort is taken—I have answered the demand with a cannon shot, & our flag still waves proudly from the walls. I shall never surrender or retreat. Then, I call on you in the name of Liberty, of patriotism & everything dear to the American character, to come to our aid, with all dispatch—The enemy is receiving reinforcements daily & will no doubt increase to three or four thousand in four or five days. If this call is neglected, I am determined to sustain myself as long as possible & die like a soldier who never forgets what is due to his own honor & that of his country—Victory or Death.

William Barret Travis
Lt. Col. comdt

P.S. The Lord is on our side—When the enemy appeared in sight we had not three bushels of corn—We have since found in deserted houses 80 or 90 bushels & got into the walls 20 or 30 head of Beeves.

Travis

Legend has it that Travis, despite the lack of reinforcements, drew a line in the sand and asked those that were willing to fight to the death to cross it. Not a single man refused.

On March 6, Santa Anna ordered a full assault on the Alamo. Within roughly one hour all Texian soldiers were killed, and those that surrendered were executed. Despite being outnumbered by almost 1,600 soldiers, the Texians managed to kill between 400 and 600 Mexican soldiers.

The few surviving women and children were allowed to live so the story of the Alamo massacre could be spread to other Texians in hopes of quelling any further revolt. As you might imagine, this had the complete opposite effect.

★　★　★　★　★　★

The Battle of San Jacinto. 1895. Painting by Henry Arthur McArdle.

FUELING THE FIRE

News of the massacres at the Alamo and Goliad served to fuel the anger among many Texians, as well as Americans in neighboring states. Soon the Texian Army's ranks began to swell under the command of General Sam Houston.

Despite the growing interest in helping the cause, Houston's plan was based on a continual retreat east to allow for time to train his rather inexperienced army. In the process of retreat he figured if they weren't gonna be able to hold the cities they passed through, they might as well burn them to the ground rather than allow Santa Anna to get his hands on them. This strategic retreat became known as the Runaway Scrape.

Unfortunately for Houston, Texians were not the retreatin' type, so he faced great resistance from his ranks. All over Texas people considered his moves to be cowardly. After much arguin' with the other government leaders, he convinced them that his plan would work if they'd only allow him to continue a little further.

INDEPENDENCE

In the meantime, at a village called Washington-on-the-Brazos, a convention was called to declare independence from Mexico. On March 2, 1836, the declaration was signed and Texas was born.

THE MASSACRE AT GOLIAD

Following the fall of the Alamo, more Texian soldiers were captured near Refugio and in the Goliad area. Despite being promised safe passage for surrendering, Santa Anna ordered their immediate execution. Over 400 soldiers, along with their leaders, William Ward and James Fannin, were executed point-blank near Mission La Bahia in Goliad.

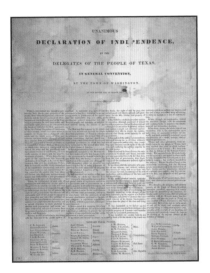

A little known fact: Several copies of the Texas Declaration of Independence had to be made because delegates kept spilling chips and queso on it.

YOU SNOOZE, YOU LOSE

At long last, General Houston had a stroke of luck that played well with his continuous retreat plan. His men intercepted a Mexican scout who had intelligence regarding the size and near-future plans of the Mexican Army. Realizing that their army was much smaller than initially thought, and that they had plans to rest for some time before continuing their pursuit of the Texian Army, General Houston rallied his troops.

With a speech in which he encouraged his men to "Remember the Alamo" and "Remember Goliad," he riled his men and urged an attack on Santa Anna's troops, who were resting in a field close by.

They rushed to find the Mexican Army on the banks of Buffalo Bayou on April 20. They spent the evening skirmishing and setting up camp. Meanwhile, Santa Anna's army continued to be reinforced, only the reinforcements were exhausted and green by all accounts.

Unfazed by the Texian army's proximity and fully expecting to squash them, Santa Anna ordered camp to be set up in what has been described as a horribly idiotic location, militarily speaking. On April 21 he ordered his men to take time to rest and relax so as to recharge and be ready for battle in the near future.

Instead, at 4:00 p.m. they were surprised by cannon shot and gunfire from the Texian army, comprising 900 soldiers. The battle was over within eighteen minutes, yet the killing of Mexican soldiers by Texians continued for hours as they shouted "Remember the Alamo" and "Remember Goliad." In broken English, many Mexican soldiers pleaded for their lives. In all, roughly 650 of the 1,300 Mexican soldiers were killed and 300 captured. On the Texian side, only eleven soldiers were lost, which if you ask me is what I'd call a whoopin'.

THANK THE LORD FOR THE YELLOW ROSE

The story goes that Santa Anna was led astray militarily by his attraction to a woman named Emily Morgan, who was an indentured servant living in the area. He was so struck by her beauty that his desire to enjoy his newfound "spoils of war" led him to set up camp in the horrible position that he did.

Some would say that Santa Anna was caught by General Houston literally with his pants down. As for Miss Emily Morgan, she lived out the rest of her life in relative peace and now lives on in Texas folklore as the woman known as the Yellow Rose of Texas.

WHERE'S SANTA ANNA?

I'm sure by now you're wonderin' what happened to General Santa Anna. He escaped briefly and tried to flee the area but was foiled by the lack of bridges over Buffalo Bayou. He donned a regular soldier's uniform to avoid bein' figured out. Unfortunately for him, when he was bein' led back into camp past his soldiers, they began to salute him, which blew his cover.

MEXICAN SURRENDER

Once Santa Anna's identity was revealed, General Houston began negotiating a surrender. Eventually an agreement was made that would have Mexico remove their soldiers from Texan soil and declare the Rio Grande as the southern border of the new Republic of Texas.

General Houston was elected the first president of this newly founded republic and all (for the most part) was well in the world. At some point in the future, Texas became part of the United States, but we won't get into that. As far as we're concerned, we're still our own country and you should consider yourself a citizen of the Republic of Texas.

The End!

(OR THE BEGINNING, DEPENDING ON HOW YOU LOOK AT IT)

A BRIEFER TIMELINE
OF TEXAS HISTORY

1000 BC:
Egyptians inscribe their pyramids with a mysterious but beautiful shape.

1609:
Galileo Galilei discovers that Earth revolves around Texas.

August 11, 1835:
Davy Crockett tells his constituents in Tennessee, "You may all go to Hell and I will go to Texas," after they choose not to reelect him.

Universe is created.

A long time ago:
Star Wars Galaxy, far away from Texas.

Some random, unimportant things took place outside of Texas.

Millions of years ago:
Dinosaurs and asteroids.

A bunch of stuff that Renaissance festivals are based on.

March 2, 1793:
Sam Houston, the first president of Texas, is born forty-three years to the day before Texas itself.

Man figures out how to ride horses and lays the foundation for what would eventually become cowboyin'.

1837:
Texas's first Tex-Mex restaurant opens.
Coincidentally, indigestion rates surge.

November 22, 1963:
Lyndon Johnson, the
first president of the
United States to be born
in Texas, is sworn in.

May 18, 1952:
George Strait
is born in
Poteet, Texas.

March 2, 1836:
Republic of Texas
is created.

1885:
Dr Pepper is
invented.

Present day:
You are reading
this book.

December 29, 1845:
Texas joins the U.S.A.
as a state. America
becomes instantly
better.

April 29, 1933:
Willie Nelson is born.

July 20, 1969:
"Houston" was the first word spoken
on the moon, followed by, "Can
you tell us if there are any good
places to get BBQ up here?"

December 28, 1838:
Current Texas flag is
adopted by the congress
of the Republic of Texas.

2

TEXAN
TRAITS

Sample Material:

FOOTBALL • THE SUN • BBQ • THE ALAMO • DRIVING A TRUCK

TEXAS PRIDE • THE MOST TEXAN NONNATIVE TEXANS

MUST BE TUFF • TEXANS VS. COWBOYS • LENDING A HAND

☆ ★ ☆ ★ ☆ ★ ☆

Us Texans are a diverse group of folks. To list a single set of unifying traits would be a task of incredible difficulty, but one that I'm more than willing to attempt. If you were to ask me what type of person belongs here, I'd say give us your loud, your proud, your huddled masses yearning to breathe the smell of brisket being smoked over a smolderin' fire of post oak. Send these, the proudest, hardest-working folks you've got, and I'll have a cold Lone Star Beer waiting for them at the border when they arrive. Search among those men and women that yearn for unlimited upward mobility. Those that find joy in the simple pleasures, like all-you-can-eat buffets and deer huntin' on a friend's ranch. Those that understand that it's hard to pull yourself up by the bootstraps when you're wearin' cowboy boots, but will try anyway. Those that understand that the bigger and taller the truck, the closer to God. We seek the individuals who can be crafted over time to mimic, adopt, and most importantly enjoy the Texan way of life with no reservations or judgment. If those that are sent here won't know what to do with all their newfound freedom, they probably won't fit in. If they're comin' with preconceived notions about how things here can be improved, they're not gonna make the cut. Send us your lovin' and friendly. Send us your happy and your humorous. Send us your toughest-built and most quick-witted folks who need some room to stretch their legs. We're here waitin' for ya at this place that we call Texas, and the place you'll soon call home. Welcome, y'all.

NOW THAT WE'VE GOTTEN THE POETRY OUT OF THE WAY . . .

A
SHORT
LIST
OF
MUSTS
FOR
ALL
TEXANS

MUST LIKE FOOTBALL

(MORE ON THIS LATER)

YOU MAY BE UNFAMILIAR WITH FOOTBALL, OR JUST NEW TO TEXAS FOOTBALL. EITHER WAY, THERE SHOULD BE AT LEAST ONE TEAM YOU CAN GET EXCITED ABOUT.

NFL

DALLAS COWBOYS   HOUSTON TEXANS

DIVISION 1 COLLEGE FOOTBALL*

UNIVERSITY OF TEXAS (LONGHORNS)
TEXAS A&M (AGGIES)
BAYLOR UNIVERSITY (BEARS)
TEXAS CHRISTIAN UNIVERSITY (HORNED FROGS)
TEXAS TECH UNIVERSITY (RED RAIDERS)
UNIVERSITY OF HOUSTON (COUGARS)
RICE UNIVERSITY (OWLS)

There are many others that should be included on this list of D1 schools. You'll also find plenty to root for in Divisions II, III, and IV.

A GENERAL GUIDE FOR WATCHING FOOTBALL*

Sunday, Monday, and Thursday: NFL
Friday: High School
Saturday: College

* The days of the week you can watch football seem to be growing, because Texans will watch football at any point, and TV execs aren't stupid.

YOU COULD CHOOSE TO SPEND YOUR TIME WATCHING THIS KIND OF FOOTBALL, BUT WHY?

HIGH SCHOOL

THERE ARE PROBABLY SEVEN GAZILLION HIGH SCHOOL TEAMS PLAYING FOOTBALL IN TEXAS. PICK ANY. THEY ALMOST ALL SERVE NACHOS.

MUST BE FRIENDLY

In general, we pride ourselves on bein' friendly folks. Being in a good overall mood is a good place to start when it comes to this trait. Any time you're feelin' down, just remember that you're now livin' in Texas. That should put some pep in your step and in the right gear for friendliness. Now that you're in an agreeable mood, here are some ways to exercise that chummy Texas charm.

OPENIN' DOORS

Despite us livin' in the twenty-first century, all doors haven't been mechanized to the point of magically openin' themselves for us. It's socially acceptable and recommended that all men make every effort to open doors for any women walkin' in or out of a door they happen to be close by. This rule extends to everyone, as a generally nice thing to do for someone else. It just ain't kind to rush through a door so fast that it swings back and hits the Texan followin' behind. If you happen to be goin' through a door, do the kind thing and look to see if anyone is followin' behind. If they are, continue to hold it open for 'em.

Stu Taylor opens door for woman that is not his wife.

LENDIN' A HAND

Openin' doors really ain't the end of it. Texans are genetically predisposed to helpin' one another. It don't matter if it's a cup of sugar or helpin' change a tire. The helpin' hand is the Texan way.

Despite losin', Chato remained friendly with the man who had just beaten him in a thumb war.

HAVIN' MANNERS

Manners are the touch of class that really make ya stand out from the herd. I've traveled everywhere and I know that some of the folks up north just do things and expect things to be done for them with no regard for anyone else. Around here we call that bein' rude.

Your first lesson in manners involves the word "please." If you'd like something done for ya, or you're askin' somethin' from someone, it's the perfect word to throw at the end of your request. "Will you be friendly, please?" See? That's not so hard.

Of course the most important part of havin' manners is simply showin' folks your appreciation for things they've done for or given to ya. To do this simple task, we employ the words "Thank you" or "Gracias" (more on that one later).

You could, for example, write a letter to me sayin', "Thank you, Jay B, for writin' what is easily the most informative book I have ever read."

Did You Know?

Bein' friendly to your fellow Texans makes you 75 percent less likely to be punched in the face or scalded with piping hot coffee? Me either. I just made this stat up.

"MMMMMMM, BRISKET."

Must Love Bar-b-que

"NOOOOOOOO, BRISKET."

MUST REMEMBER THE ALAMO

IN TEXAS, THE ALAMO IS CONSIDERED SACRED GROUND. IT'S WHERE A FEW HUNDRED MEN AND WOMEN GAVE THEIR LIVES TO ENSURE THAT THE REST OF US COULD LIVE IN THE GREATEST OF ALL REPUBLICS. "REMEMBER THE ALAMO" AIN'T JUST A SAYING FOR TOURIST KEYCHAINS. IT'S A REQUIREMENT.

THE BATTLE OF THE ALAMO		
	BELLIGERENTS	
	Mexico	Republic of Texas
ARMY SIZE	1,800	185–257
CASUALTIES	~500	182–257

Did You Know?

The Alamo was built in 1744 by the Catholic Church as a mission. The chapel was eventually sold to the state of Texas for $20,000 in 1883.

MUST NOT BE FLAMMABLE

Texas has a full 482 days a year of intense sunshine.
Highly flammable folks need not apply.

IN THE CASE OF SUN-INDUCED SPONTANEOUS COMBUSTION:

1. REMAIN CALM.

2. CALL 911.

3. ADVISE THEM ON WHERE TO LOCATE YOUR CHARRED BODY.

4. HANG UP PHONE.

5. RUN WHILE WAVING YOUR ARMS AS FAST AS POSSIBLE TO ATTEMPT TO PUT OUT FLAMES.

6. LOCATE NEAREST POOL.

7. JUMP IN NEAREST POOL.*

*DON'T DO ANY OF THIS. STOP, DROP, AND ROLL.

MUST BE ABLE TO DRIVE A TRUCK
(OR BE CAPABLE OF LEARNIN')

Excited about driving a truck

Let 'er rip

Driving a truck while being
all business

Hitting on ladies, but forgetting
you left your hard hat on

Teaching your son how to hit on
ladies with a hard hat on

Driving a truck you "won"
at the rodeo

Driving a truck while
yelling at hoodlums

The safe way of texting when
driving a truck

Not currently driving,
but plenty capable

MUST BE PRIDEFUL

Texans aren't anything if not prideful. We'll take credit for dang near anything and attempt to outdo anything that's already been done. We built the tallest building in the world. The San Jacinto Monument in La Porte, Texas, stands as a testament to the men who fought and won Texas's independence on that ground. It's a real beauty.

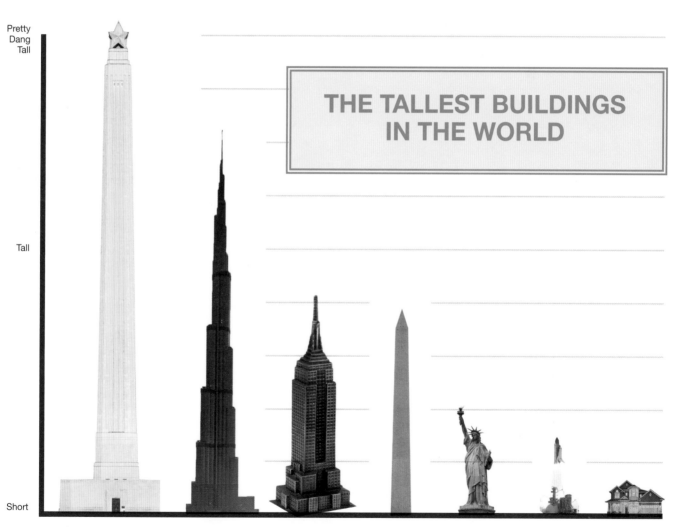

THE TALLEST BUILDINGS IN THE WORLD

Pretty Dang Tall — Tall — Short

San Jacinto Monument, La Porte, TX

Burj Khalifa, Dubai, UAE

Empire State Building, New York, NY

Washington Monument, Washington, DC

Statue of Liberty, New York, NY

Space shuttle

Home, Anytown, USA

MUST BE ABLE TO CLAP IN THE EVENT THAT SOMEONE YELLS,

THE STARS AT NIGHT,

ARE BIG AND BRIGHT,

DEEP IN THE HEART OF TEXAS

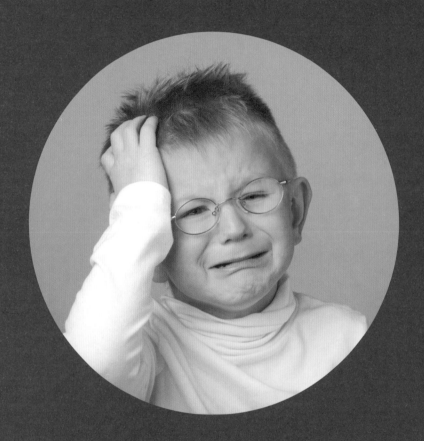

MUST FREAK OUT
WHEN IT RAINS

MUST GET HERE QUICKLY
IF NOT ALREADY HERE

We have a saying around Texas that goes "Lucky to be American. Blessed to be Texan." The common misconception is that to be true Texan, you must be born here. Although it'll win you extra credibility points, it's by no means necessary. In fact, some of the most Texan of all Texans weren't from around here at all. Davy Crockett, Stephen F. Austin, and Sam Houston were all born outside of Texas. All that matters is that you get here as fast as you can.

MUST BE

Barbed wire is commonly used to show toughness (see bars, bumper stickers, koozies, etc.).

TUFF

Ultimately if you're gonna survive in Texas, above all you've gotta have a certain toughness to ya. We love the slice of heaven that we call home, but we'll be the first to tell ya that during some of the summer months, it can be hell on Earth. The following is a snippet from "Hell in Texas" that will explain what I mean:

The devil was given permission one day
To make him a land for his own special sway.
He scattered tarantulas over roads.
Put thorns on the cactus and horns on
    the toads.
He lengthened the horns of the Texas steer
And added a foot to the jackrabbit's ear.
He hung thorns and brambles on all the
    trees,
He mixed up the dust with a million fleas.
He quickened the buck of the bronco steed,
And poisoned the feet of the centipede.
The heat in the summer's a hundred and ten,
Too hot for the devil and too hot for men.

In case you haven't figured it out by now, one of the many things we have ample supply of is sunlight. That bein' the case, you don't need to be wealthy to live in Texas, but you do need to be able to afford sunscreen. Life without it will be miserable for you. Even the most

Texas in August

seasoned Texan has on occasion forgotten to wear it, so don't beat yourself up the first time you do. After you finish gawking at your new lobster-like state in the mirror, just take a bath in aloe vera lotion and remember that I told you so.

Also bear in mind that no one is impressed by the folks who claim that they "don't need sunscreen." We've seen it a thousand times. Don't try to prove your toughness by venturing into the blistering heat without protection. You'll end up

a blistered heap.

As for the heat that comes along with the overabundance of sunshine, one of my favorite old sayings goes, "If you can't stand the heat, get out of Texas." It's absolutely true. If your name starts with "Frosty" and ends with "Snowman," our climate might be a severe detriment to your quality of life. "Heat waves" of 85°+ weather may be something to be scared of in the rest of the country, but they're nothing to pay much attention to around here. Frankly, we consider ourselves lucky when we're graced with 90° weather.

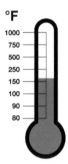

To say it's just plain hot is to simplify the state too much. In the East, it's hot and humid. There's a humidity there so thick that you need a well-sharpened Bowie knife to cut through it.

In the West, it's hot, dry, and windy.

That may not sound scary, but I assure you that no amount of lotion is gonna do you good. Spend a short amount of time out there and you'll look like a fifty-three-year-old leather bag.

Like we covered earlier, our seasons all tend to be pretty hot, so you'd better just get used to the feeling of spontaneous combustion—it's inescapable for the most part. Don't get all overwhelmed if this information is comin' as a surprise. We've perfected the science of coolin' off.

Air conditioning will help your chances of survival—even the most Antarctic among you. If you're still feeling like it may overwhelm your internal cooling capabilities, just grab one of our numerous delicious Texas beers out of the many refrigerators strategically placed throughout the state.

They'll give you the final cooling boost you'll need to keep from burnin' up.

If the sunburns and heat-strokes don't kill ya, the wildlife and plants might. Basically, if it grows out of the ground or has feet and walks on it, it'll poke or bite ya.

Taken together, all of this would paint a pretty horrible picture for what it's like to live in Texas. What you can't forget though is Texans generally like a challenge, and the idea of livin' somewhere that just ain't made for the weakhearted is exactly the kinda place a Texan wants to hang their hat.

MUST CHOOSE SIDES

This may be the granddaddy of all subjective topics in Texas. All Texans like football. Those that don't just lie and say they do so they fit in. For our purposes we're just gonna pretend those people don't exist.

That bein' said, everyone has an opinion on whether they like the Dallas Cowboys or the Houston Texans. Honestly, you don't have to like either, but you've gotta have a stance. Once you do, feel free to throw it out in casual conversation.

MUST TAKE CHEESY BLUEBONNET
PHOTO EVERY SPRING

NON-TEXAN THINGS
AND
HABITS TO LEAVE AT THE DOOR

We don't mind the folks moving here havin' a bit of diversity. Heck, a big part of what makes Texas a great place in the first place is the melting pot of cultures and habits folks from various places have brought with 'em over the years. That bein' said, there are some things and habits you'll want to leave behind. Some are so you'll survive the environment, others are so you'll survive the people.

First off, you'll want to lose whatever leave-me-alone attitude you might have picked up, ahem, up north. 'Round here, we're friendly with folks we've never met. Sayin' "howdy" (or "hello," if you're still gettin' used to how we speak), "please," and "thank you" are all common courtesies for anyone you see, including strangers. In other places this is called Southern hospitality. Here, it's called bein' friendly and polite. We don't need an excuse to do it just because we're in the South. We do it because we're born this way. Not followin' this advice will result in other Texans forever mistakin' you for someone born in New York. Save yourself the trouble and get friendly before you get across our borders.

Numero dos on our list of things to leave behind would be any incredibly heavy winter clothing. This one is optional in that you're welcome to bring it if you'd like, but it's doubtful you'll wear it much. The four seasons we normally experience around here are called sorta summer, definitely summer, kinda summer, and not summer, the last of which is the season all y'all would normally wear this type of layered clothin'. It's what y'all might call a mild winter. When it gets a little chilly here you might layer up to stave off the cold, but I recommend against it. With the way the weather changes here you're liable to bake to death before you can layer down, so just go ahead and leave this clothing at home.

We'll cover the Texan language in further detail in the future, but for now I would say that you should leave horrible habits like calling your coke "pop" and saying "you all" or "you guys" at the border. In Texas all sodas are "cokes" and Dr Pepper is "Dr Pepper." "Y'all" is a word that I'm sure you're aware of and will quickly become proficient at using. I assure you we will make you proficient in short order, but until then, just believe me and leave those habits at the door.

We appreciate that y'all did things in a certain manner where you're from. In fact, in the privacy of your own home it's your business to continue to do so. Just know that in public there are few Texans who will care about your previous non-Texan life. We find it crass and impolite to suggest that there are better ways than doing things the way things are done here.

If you're a health nut, you should leave your diet at home. We've got the only diet you'll ever need. It's called the Texan diet. You can eat whatever you want. That's it. Seriously, that's the diet. Other than those few minor things, you're all set.

3

TALKIN' TEXAN

Sample Material:

IT ISN'T "HI," IT'S "HOWDY" • LEAVIN' OFF THE "G" • A GUIDE TO USING "Y'ALL"
"FIXIN'" VS. "GOING TO" • "AIN'T" • PHRASES THAT ARE PRETTY MUCH WORDS
COUNTIN' & UNITS OF MEASUREMENT • SPANGLISH • TOPICS OF DISCUSSION
HOW TO ENGAGE WITH FOREIGNERS

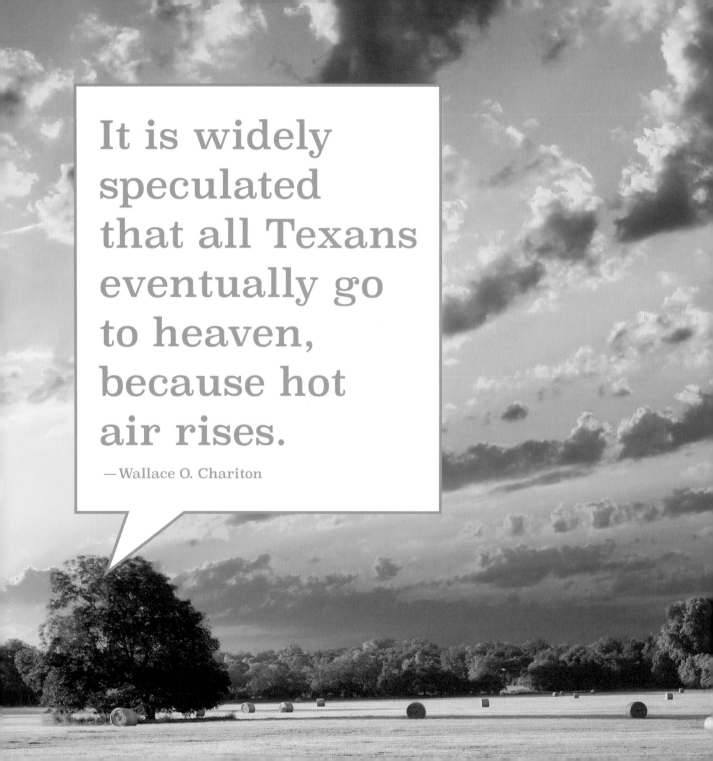

The Texas language is a complex, constantly changin' thing. It has evolved during my lifetime alone. It's made up of words and expressions borrowed from the numerous cultures that have at one time or another called Texas home. Despite the amalgamated nature of our talk, the complexity of our communicatin' shouldn't scare you. It'll be fairly easy for you to pick up given some patience, a couple of beers, and a slight disregard for what you were taught in school.

BEGINNER TALKIN' TEXAN

We'll start with a few ground rules to get you off the ground and runnin'.

WE DON'T SAY "HI"— WE SAY "HOWDY"

You may or may not know this, but "howdy" is a contraction of the words "how do you do." It also just sounds a heck of a lot nicer without sounding too much like a Northerner. Anyway, we don't really say "hi" or "hello" to anyone. "Howdy" should be substituted for any of those words.

THE "G" IN THE "-ING" OF SPOKEN WORDS IS SILENT, AND IT'S LEFT OFF WHEN WRITTEN

When it comes to pronunciation and spellin' of verbs that end in "-ing," the letter "n" and the apostrophe are your best friends. Where you come from, the "ing" sound is what you probably expect to hear at the end of words like "going," "flying," and "eating." In Texas, "in" is all you'll be hearin'.

Don't take this rule as a sign that Texans are a lazy bunch. It's all about bein' efficient while speakin'. We just prefer to work smarter, not harder.

LEAVIN' THE "G" OUT OF IT

We're gonna go to the swimmin' hole after a while. If you're wantin' to come, you'd best be gettin' ready, y'all.

I'm fixin' ta get supper goin'. If y'all 'er hungry, I can start servin' some chips and salsa for ya to snack on before.

Shootin' the gun is the easy part. It's the cleanin' of the deer afterwards that my wife don't enjoy.

Notice in the above examples the verbs are what we drop the last "g" from, but in the case of the word "things," it stays. As with most language rules, this one is made to be broken occasionally. Kinda like "i" before "e," except in the case of "Budweiser."

DO NOT DARE UTTER THE PHRASE "YOU ALL" IN TEXAS—"Y'ALL" IS YOUR NEW FRIEND

This one is incredibly important, and although it's used in other regions of the South, we take a lot of pride in its usage right here in Texas. It's our way of sayin' "you guys" or "all of you."

It's not one size fits y'all, though. When you're talkin' to one person, you still should use the word "you." When addressin' two folks, go ahead and fire up that good, deep "y'all." For three or more folks though, add in an "all" to your "y'all," for a nice, round "all y'all" and you'll be grammatically correct. See the figure on the facing page for a quick visual reference.

ALL SODAS ARE "COKES"

I've been told by folks who have traveled to foreign lands such as New York and Michigan that the natives of those regions like to call their sodas "pop." I can't speak from experience because I've never been north of the Red River. What I can speak at ya is that doin' so here will be cause for much confusion. Generally speakin', if you were to ask for a "pop," someone might think you were askin' to be hit upside the head, or for your father. If you'd like a soda of some sort, simply start by asking, "May I please have a coke?" Whomever you just asked this of will then reply, "Sure thing. What kind?" This is the point at

which you'd answer more specifically. If you did in fact want a Coca-Cola, you'd simply reply back, "Coke is fine." If you wanted anything else, you'd specify.

The only caveat to this rule is that all sodas are cokes, but not all cokes are Dr Pepper. If you'd prefer to drink Dr Pepper, just ask for that right off the bat and save everyone a ton of time.

Dr Pepper is the oldest soft drink in the United States. It even predates Coca-Cola, as it was developed in the 1880s and made its debut in 1885.

YOU AREN'T "GOING TO" DO ANYTHING—YOU'RE "FIXIN' TO"

The phrase "fixin' to" is what we like to call the national verb of Texas. It serves two roles in our language. It helps us express either our intention to do somethin' or describes somethin' we are about to do in the very near future. Masterin' the usage of this verb phrase will ensure safe passage throughout much of the South, as we are not the only ones to put it to good use.

> **"**
> I'M FIXIN'
> TO FIX THIS DAMN
> DISPOSAL.
> **"**

BOWIE KNIVES

I am quite familiar with the famous British singer named David Bowie. I'm also familiar with the fact that he liked to have his name pronounced *boh'-wee*. Well I'll warn you right away that around here the name Bowie is pronounced *boo'-wee*. I don't care if it "doesn't look like it's pronounced that way."

Remember what I told you earlier. Leave your preconceived notions or ideas about how you used to do things at the door and listen to me.

DIRECTIONS DON'T MATTER

At any point throughout your day, someone might direct you to come on down, come on up, or come on over. Where you're currently located relative to them don't really matter. They're basically askin' you to come to them, regardless of the direction.

A GUIDE TO UNDERSTANDING Y'ALL

YOU

ONE PERSON

Y'ALL

TWO PEOPLE

ALL Y'ALL

THREE OR MORE PEOPLE

INTERMEDIATE TALKIN' TEXAN

Now that you've gotten the run-of-the-mill basics out of the way, it's time to delve into the words and phrases that will make people think you might actually be from here. These aren't hard to grasp, but they do require a bit of finesse to use smoothly.

AIN'T

"Ain't" is the best place to start. It's a simple contraction of the words "am not," "are not," "is not," "have not," and "has not." Some of the scholarly types like to say that it ain't correct English to use the word "ain't" in a sentence. Well, they ain't the boss of me or the president of Texas, so what they have to say just ain't holdin' water as far as I'm concerned.

This word is an easy one in the sense that you don't have to change it, regardless of how it's bein' used. Over time, you'll understand what words the "ain't" is contraction'in for in the sentence you hear it in. Just listen for the context clues. Look at the examples on the right to see what I mean.

USIN' AIN'T

I ain't lyin'!
I am not lying!

I ain't gone there before.
I have not been there before.

You ain't goin' to the bar tonight!
You are not going to the bar tonight!

He/She ain't from around here?
He/She is not from around here?

They ain't gonna tell me how to mow my lawn!
They are not going to mow my lawn.

We ain't gonna drink no fancy beers.
We are not going to drink fancy beers.

If it ain't broke, don't fix it.
If it is not broken, don't fix it.

 TEXAN TALK   NORMAL ENGLISH

WORDS YOU'VE NEVER SEEN BEFORE, OR THAT HAVE ALTERNATE MEANIN'S

Biggo (adjective)—Describes something that is large. A shortening of the words "big 'ol." Example: "I argued with the man, but I wasn't tryin' to get in no fistfight. He was a biggo dude."

Folk (noun)—A word used to describe a group of people. Not to be confused with "folk," which is a type of music. Can be used in its singular or plural form to refer to groups of Texans. Example: "Those Williamsons are just good plain folks." "You know, I always liked the Cantus. They're some good folk."

Gussied up (adjective)—The state of being nicer lookin' than you would normally, either by way of showering, clothing, or just plain not lookin' like you just fell off the farm truck. Example: "Juan heard that his ex-girlfriend was comin' to the beer joint tonight, so he took a shower so he could get all gussied up."

Looker (noun)—Someone who is considered to be very good lookin' relative to the rest of the population. Example: "Have you seen John's sister Debbie? She's quite the looker."

King George is considered a looker in these parts.

'Nuther (adjective) / nuh'-ther—A shortenin' of the word "another."

Beer   'Nuther Beer

On'ry (adjective) / on'-ree—Being in an angry and agitated state. Example: "I wouldn't go in there and talk to her. She's been actin' on'ry ever since Mom told her that she couldn't go to the lake this weekend with Todd."

Supper (noun)—A word used to describe dinner in Texas. Example: "Let's head on back to the house and have ourselves a big supper. Whaddya say?"

Tank (noun)—A hole in the ground that with adequate rain fills with water and sometimes houses fish. In other regions this is known as a pond. Example: "I went fishin' this mornin' up at the tank. They sure were bitin', but I couldn't hook a single one."

Tump (verb)—The process of knocking or flipping something over from its upright position. Example: "Hey Bubba, will you go tump that bucket of rainwater over so we don't get mosquitos?"

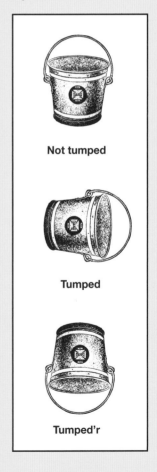

Not tumped

Tumped

Tumped'r

PHRASES THAT ARE PRETTY MUCH WORDS

All worked up (adjective)—Used to describe someone who's pretty ticked off about somethin'. Example: "He's gettin' himself all worked up over that dang speedin' ticket, but no one was makin' him speed. He shoulda slowed down."

Cattywampus (adjective) / cad'-dee-wom'-pus—A word to describe when something just ain't right lookin'. It can be broken, off-kilter, or just plain weird. Example: "I saw Blue the other day walkin' down the street and he was all disheveled. His jeans were stained, his shirt had holes in it, and his hat was on his head sideways all cattywampus like. It was weird."

Do what (interjection)—Can be used in place of sayin' "pardon me" when you don't hear what someone said to you. Example: "Hey Bobby, did you hear what I said?" "No, do what?"

Eaten up (verb)—A phrase used to describe being bitten a lot by the large nearly mammal-like mosquitos that we have throughout our state. Example: "I would have had a great time at the BBQ, but I was too busy gettin' eaten up by the mosquitos."

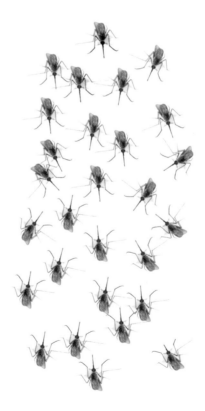

Lester Skeeter and his many friends. Bloodthirsty savages.

Get down (verb)—A phrase used to signify the process of getting out of a vehicle once you've arrived at your destination. Example: "When we get to the corner store, is anyone else gonna get down with me and grab somethin' from inside? If not, I can get down by myself."

Hissy fit (noun)—A respectable-sized tantrum or outburst thrown by someone that everyone else in the vicinity can tell is completely overblown. Example: "No, I left Brandon at home because he was throwin' a hissy fit that I wouldn't let him bring his dog, Tex, with him. It was ridiculous."

Howdy'd (verb)—A verb form of the word "howdy" that refers to the act of meeting or bein' formally introduced to them. Example: "I've seen him around the shop before, but we still haven't howdy'd."

Lit out (verb)—To leave a location extremely quickly without regard for sayin' goodbye. Example: "After Tammy gave the ring he gave her back to him, he hopped in his Ram and lit outta here like a bat outta hell."

Might could (adverb)—Describes something that can possibly or maybe be. Example: "I've never ridden a bull before, but give me enough beers and I might could do it."

Hissy fits come in all shapes and sizes. See page 74 for the definition if you've never been around another human or animal.

Plug ugly (adjective)—Describes something or someone as being less than attractive by normal standards. Generally used for something that is by all accounts just bad lookin'. Example: "Look, I appreciate you settin' me up with your best friend for that date, but honestly he was just plug ugly. I can't date someone that looks like that."

Pony up (verb)—To speed up or give something more effort. Example: "If she's gonna hang with the rest of that team for this game, she'd better pony up right quick."

Ridin' high (adjective)—See "Walkin' in tall cotton."

Right quick (adverb)—To do something very rapidly or soon. Example: "Hey, man, I need some help movin' these cinder blocks under the trailer. It'll only take a second though. Will you help me right quick?"

Tellin' a windy (verb)—A phrase for describin' the act of lyin'. Its roots are based in the concept of someone bein' full of hot air. Example: "Look, I just don't think you really saw a chupacabra. I think you're tellin' a windy."

Tuckered out (adjective)—Describes someone bein' extremely exhausted and in a sleeping or resting state. Most often used with regard to kids who have spent all their energy. Example: "Little Cody Larry is a tired man. He's been wrestlin' with Buzz all day. He's been tuckered out on the couch since five."

Walkin' in tall cotton (adjective)—Used to describe someone who is rich or has had a lot of personal success. Example: "Man, by the looks of the cars he's drivin', and the meals he's eatin' and postin' about on Instagram, that guy must be walkin' in tall cotton."

"Oh, you think that's crazy? Wait 'til you hear this latest story that nobody here will believe."
—Kevin Windy

This image showed up when searching for "tall cotton." No idea how this fits, but these folks seem to be doin' fine, so it'll do.

ADVANCED TALKIN' TEXAN

The hardest part about learnin' to talk Texan isn't learnin' all the words. It's the conversin' with other Texans part of conversatin'. Texans can pick out a fake from a mile away, so the pronunciations and use of random metaphors is key to fittin' in with your new Texas brethren.

Pronouncin' things correctly in Texan rarely involves pronouncin' based on the way the word looks. Following are some pronunciations of words that people have a history of gettin' wrong. They're all fairly easy to pick up. Once you master these, you'll pick up the rest by trial and error (and by undoubtedly gettin' corrected by Texans repeatedly).

PLACES WORTH KNOWING HOW TO SAY RIGHT

Abilene	ab'-uh-leen	**Carrizo Springs**	cuh-ree'-zo springs
Alamo	al'-uh-mo	**Chisholm**	chiz'-uhm
Amarillo	am-uh-ril'-o	**Cibolo**	see-bo'-low
Aransas	uh-ran'-sus	**Fulshear**	full'-sher
Austin	aws'-stun	**Gruene**	green
Balmorhea	ball'-muh-ray	**Guadalupe**	gwad-ah-loop'-aye
Bandera	ban-dare'-uh	**Helotes**	eh-lote'-ess
Bertram	burr'-trum	**Joaquin**	wok-een'
Bexar	bay'-err or bear	**Mexia**	muh-hi'-uh
Blanco	blang'-co	**New Braunfels**	new brahn'-felz
Boerne	burn'-knee	**Palacios**	puh-lash'-us
Bonham	bahn'-mm	**Palestine**	pal'-uh-steen
Bowie	boo'-wee	**Refugio**	ref-yoo'-ee-oh
Brookshire	brook'-sher	**Waxahachie**	wawks-uh-hatch'-eeh
Budah	byooh'-duh	**Ysleta**	Yeehs-let'-uh
Burnet	burn'-it		

SAYIN' IT BY SAYIN' SOMETHIN' ELSE

There are as many metaphors, hyperbole, and idioms bein' used in Texas as there are heads of cattle in this state. Master this portion of our language and you'd be ready to run for office in our great state without anyone even knowin' you're a former foreigner.

A senseless tragedy.

COUNTIN' AND UNITS OF MEASUREMENT

When you're tryin' to describe the size of things to people, it's a very Texan thing to do to use other states as units of measurement. For example, when describin' the King Ranch in South Texas, we often compare it to the puny state of Rhode Island. I suggest attempting to do the same yourself in random conversation.

With regard to quantities of various things, any of these phrases below would be perfect for use.

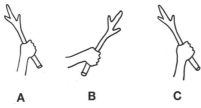

A **B** **C**

More than you can shake a stick at—A large quantity of whatever it is that's being described. Example: "Down at the flea market you'll find more belt buckles than you can shake a stick at."

Frog strangler—This phrase describes a large amount of rain. An amount so large it would potentially drown an animal that finds itself generally adept in the water. Example: "That rainstorm just sat over the area for most of the night. It dumped a heck of a lotta rain. It was a real frog strangler." (See also "Gully washer" and "Turd floater.")

Gully washer—A description of a massive amount of rainfall. Refers to the flushing through of a normally dry or muddy gully or stream. Example: "That was a heck of a storm last night. It was a certified gully washer, if you ask me."

Turd floater—Used to describe a storm that dumped so much rain that it can cause some plumbing problems in areas with less-than-modern sewer systems. Example: "That storm looks like it's goin' to be a real turd floater with all the rain it's gonna drop."

Swimmin' in it—Used to describe when someone is overwhelmed by something. Example: "Man, I talked to Charlie the other day and he sounded like they're super busy with that new project down in Taylor. He's swimmin' in it these days."

All hat, no cattle—Describes someone who is seemingly all for show and not made up of much substance. Also used to describe someone who is "full of it." Example: "Don't believe a word that guy tells you about how to buy a truck. He doesn't know what he's talkin' about. He's all hat, no cattle."

Ridin' a gravy train with biscuit wheels—One of the oddest sayings us Texans have, this one describes the comfy lifestyle or easy time someone is having due to their blessed circumstances. This one makes no sense, but sounds pretty darn good. Example: "Juan's kids don't have to do much of anything these days now that Juan struck oil on his land. Those kids have got it good, man. They are ridin' a gravy train with biscuit wheels."

DESCRIBIN' THINGS AND PEOPLE

Any of the phrases below can be used to help convey various aspects of a person or a thing with a lot of emphasis.

Madder than a wet hen—Compares someone's anger to the anger level of a wet, nonwaterfaring barnyard animal common on many Texas farms. Example: "When I told my wife that I scratched her Cadillac with the brush guard on my truck, she got madder than a wet hen."

He's as welcome as a skunk at a lawn party—No one likes skunks. Period. Example: "We were so pissed that he invited himself over to the house. We all made him feel about as welcome as a skunk at a lawn party."

I wouldn't trust him any farther than I can throw him—Used to compare one's inability to throw a full-sized human being far with the metaphorical amount they'd trust them. Example: "That guy has been lyin' to everyone he knows. I wouldn't trust him any farther than I could throw him."

He'd foul up a two-car funeral procession—Refers to the simplicity and uncomplicated nature of a small funeral procession and describes the individual's propensity to, despite the simplicity, still figure out a way to screw it up. Example: "You can't trust her to do anything right. She'd foul up a two-car funeral procession."

She's got enough tongue for ten rows of teeth—Used in instances where someone wants to describe the talkative nature of a particular person. Example: "You couldn't get a word in with Jessica. She talked the entire dang night! She's got enough tongue for ten rows of teeth."

He was runnin' like the dogs were after him—Refers to the quick speed you'd need to be runnin' to outpace a pack of huntin' dogs. Example: "Brian sure was quick to get outside when they told him his truck was bein' towed. He was runnin' like the dogs were after him."

He looks like the dog's been keepin' him under the porch—Used to describe someone who isn't the most handsome or pretty person around. Example: "That fella is plug ugly. He looks like the dog's been keepin' him under the porch."

"Hey guys, what time's the party on Saturday?"

"What party?"

"Should we save some for Geoff?"

"Screw him. He's from Oklahoma."

About as friendly as fire ants—A description used for someone who isn't particularly friendly to others. Example: "I keep runnin' into Mr. Randy and he is just so mean. He's about as friendly as fire ants."

She was lookin' at me like a calf looks at a new gate—Baby cows, also known as calves, can be easily confused by things they don't understand. Gates and fences fall in that category. This saying references that fact. Example: "I didn't mean to confuse her, but when I told her about it, she looked at me like a calf looks at a new gate."

You're as happy as a gopher in soft dirt—For the unaware, gophers spend a lot of their time diggin' tunnels, so it would make sense that they like soft dirt. Example: "When I brought over the tres leches cake, she was happier than a gopher in soft dirt."

That man is tighter than bark on a tree—Used to describe how tight with their money a particular person is. Example: "Don't even ask Gerald to contribute to the present we're gonna buy for Tammy. When it comes to spendin' money, that guy is tighter than bark on a tree."

Wasn't me.

Fred, the liar horse

They're as full of wind as a corn-eatin' horse—Used to describe someone who seems to be full of hot air. Being that horses are meant to eat grass and aren't exactly known for their stable digestive system, corn-eating horses tend to be on the gassy side of the spectrum. Example "I don't buy a single thing she tells me. She's as full of wind as a corn-eatin' horse."

The engine's runnin' but ain't nobody drivin'—Describes an individual who is not someone people would call intelligent. Example: "I've tried to explain to your son a thousand times that just because some guy on TV asks for a donation don't mean that he's gotta send one in. Sometimes I think his engine's runnin' but there just ain't nobody drivin'."

GIVIN' ADVICE

The next few phrases are perfect for givin' that random person you're talkin' to at the moment the perfect piece of metaphorical advice that they need to get them through whatever is eatin' 'em.

Nobody ever drowned in sweat—Used to express to someone that hard work is a good thing and has never killed anyone. Example: "Bobby, stop complainin' about the yardwork. Helpin' out around the house now and then is good for ya. Nobody ever drowned in sweat. You'll be fine."

Don't be a hundred-dollar saddle and a twenty-dollar horseman—Expresses the need for people to keep their priorities straight by comparing the ridiculousness of someone spending a lot of money on a saddle when they don't even know the basics of horsemanship. Example: "Hector is a nice guy and all, but he seems to be all show and doesn't know much about what he's doin'. He's got a hundred-dollar saddle even though he's a twenty-dollar horseman."

You can put boots in the oven, but it don't make 'em biscuits—A description of the fact that situations are what they are and can't be changed just by willin' them to change alone. Example: "Look, Peter, your wife left you. Just because you're tellin' yourself that she's comin' back don't mean she is. You can put boots in the oven, but it don't make 'em biscuits."

Throwin' a rope 'fore you make a loop ain't gonna catch the cow—A metaphor explaining that proper planning is necessary for anything to go well. Example: "Son, just because you eyeballed the length of the board doesn't mean it was gonna be right. That's why you cut the thing too short. Throwin' a rope 'fore you make a loop ain't gonna catch the cow."

"I take offense to this joke. I've been ridin' horses for years, and hell, the saddle was only forty bucks."

—Hector

EMPHASIZIN'

The last batch of sayin's are particularly good at emphasis and randomness. Some are just polite.

I'll tell you what—A phrase that serves as less of a metaphor and more of a "teeing up" or emphasizing whatever phrase came before it or comes after it. Examples: "I'll tell you what . . . if my boss cuts my hours again, he's gonna get an earful from me." "Man, she was a good-lookin' girl, I'll tell you what."

The face often used when starting with "I'll tell you what."

Bless your heart—A phrase used to imply that you feel bad for someone, even if you don't. Can also be used to kindly tell someone to go to hell. The actual meaning behind its use is generally only evident to the person uttering it. Examples: "Oh, you're not from Texas? Bless your heart." "You think you're better than me? Bless your heart."

DOUBLE CONTRACTIONS

On occasion, we find it easier and better soundin' to contractionize three words. I know that in other places where folks speak "proper" English, this is looked down upon. Well, here we look down on everyone else that ain't Texan anyway, so the feelin' is mutual. We'll start with the word "y'all" as a basis.

Y'ALL

As you remember, the word "y'all" is a contraction of the words "you" and "all." With double contractions, you can save yourself boatloads of time by taggin' on an extra word. Examples:

Y'ALL EXAMPLES

Y'all're—*You all are*
Y'all's—*The possessive form of "y'all"*
Y'all've—*You all have*
Y'all'll—*You all will*
Y'all'd—*You all would / you all had*

OTHERS

There are many others that will come up over time, but these are the most used from what I've found. Acquaint yourself with them and the next time some Texan is slurrin' his words or chicken scratchin' what they're wantin' to say on paper, you'll've already been brought up to speed.

OTHER EXAMPLES

He'd've / She'd've—*He should have / she should have*
He'don't / She'don't—*He does not / she does not*
I'd've—*I would have*
I'll've—*I will have*
Couldn't've—*Could not have*
Shouldn't've—*Should not have*
Wouldn't've—*Would not have*
That'll've—*That will have*
Mustn't've—*Must not have*

TRIPLE AND QUADRUPLE CONTRACTIONS

In the rarest of occasions, there's an opportunity to contraction-ize four or more words into a triple or quadruple contraction. They truly show off the power that is the word "y'all."

CONTRACTIONIZ'N

Y'all'd've—*You all would have*
Y'all'd'nt—*You all would not*
Y'all'd'nt've—*You all would not have*

I'M GONNA SPANK YOU WITH A CHANCLA.

NO PISE EL GRASS

SPANGLISH

Texan culture is influenced by all of the cultures that surround our sovereign republic. Over the years the Native Americans, Cajuns, Germans, Czech, French, Spanish, and Mexicans have all made major contributions to the flavors in the Texan melting pot. When it comes to language, though, the Spanish and Mexican influence is incredibly strong.

The names of many of our roads, regions, and rivers alone are evident of this exact fact. Over time, we've borrowed the Spanish equivalent of English words and used them interchangeably. This amalgamation of languages is what we like to call Spanglish. Depending on where in Texas you are, it can be made up of 90 percent English and 10 percent Spanish, or 90 percent Spanish and 10 percent English (if you're in the Rio Grande Valley). For the purposes of just gettin' you up to speed with bein' a

Texan, we won't dive into how to speak Spanish, because honestly, I took four years of high school Spanish and that still wasn't enough for me to be fluent. What we will do is make you proficient in the basics of Spanglish so you're not thrown for a total loop the next time you're hit with words that are completely foreign to folks like yourself.

The first thing you need to know is that there's no rhyme or reason to when or how someone decides to interject Spanish or English words into their speech. If someone is speakin' Spanglish, it is entirely up to the speaker to decide how much or little of either to insert. In some instances the seemingly Spanish word is actually an English word with a Spanish-sounding pronunciation. Below is a list of a few words so you can get acquainted with the concept.

PARKING CON PERMISO SOLAMENTE

Chanclas sporting the red, white, and blue. Great for toobin' on the Fourth of July.

EXAMPLES OF SPANGLISH WORDS

Washateria *(laundromat)*
Takes the English word "wash" and adds the Spanish suffix "-teria" to the end of it.

Sanwich *(sandwich)*
This word is more of a pronunciation than it is a brand new word. The English word "sandwich" has the "d" dropped and leaves the remainder to be pronounced, one caveat being that the last "ch" sound is pronounced as "shhhh."

Lonche *(lunch)*
The English word is morphed into a Spanish-sounding version. Replaces the word almuerzo, which is the correct Spanish term.

Wacha *(to watch or look)*
The English word "watch" is transformed by droppin' the "t" and addin' an "a."

Parkear *(to park)*
The English word "park" is transformed into a Spanish verb by adding an "-ar" to the end, which normally signifies a verb in Spanish.

Now that we've covered the individual words that look like Spanish but are definitely Spanglish, we can talk about the blend of languages and how to make sense of them. It's simple really. Assuming English was your first language, if you see a word that you don't recognize, it's probably Spanish. If you don't understand the majority of the sentence but you recognize an English word or two, you're probably in South Texas. A few examples are in the box at right.

EXAMPLES OF SPANGLISH PHRASES

"¿Estas ready?" *("Are you ready?")*

"Pues, you'd better behave or I'm gonna spank you with a chancla."
("Well, you'd better behave or I'm gonna spank you with a sandal.")

"¡Vámonos a lonche!" *("Let's go to lunch!")*

"Juan, por qué no estas parkear here?"
("Juan, why not park here?")

TEXAN TOPICS OF DISCUSSION

Right off the bat, you may not have a lot in common with the Texans who have been livin' here
for a long time, and that's okay. It's to be expected that it'll take some time for
you to get up to speed on things to talk about with your fellow Texans. In the meantime, here
are a few subjects that can be used to strike up a conversation with pretty much any Texan
you might encounter.

SECESSION

Nothin' gets Texans fired up like discussin' how awesome
it would be if we were our own country again. We were
once, so why not one more time, right?

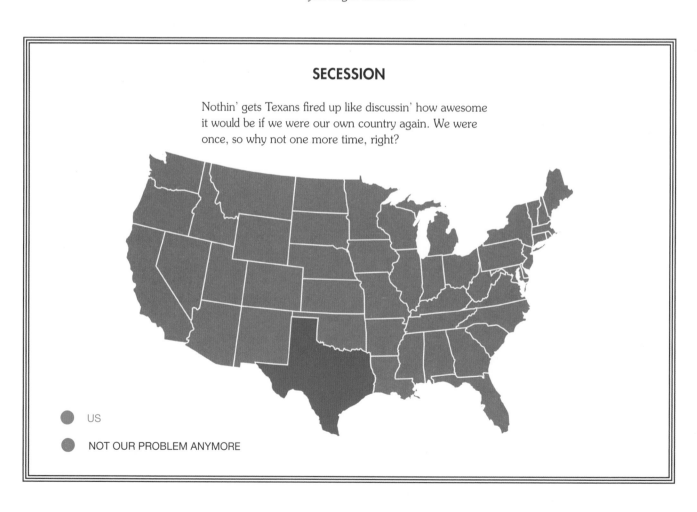

US

NOT OUR PROBLEM ANYMORE

HOW AWESOME/ WEIRD AUSTIN IS

It won't take long for you to figure out how different Austin is from the rest of the state. It's a great city with a lot of fantastic food and things to do outdoors, but it's just weird compared to the rest of our cities. Maybe it's because they have a birthday party for the fictional Eeyore from *Winnie the Pooh*, or it might have somethin' to do with the guy who rides his bike in a thong through downtown every day like it's no big deal.

When it comes to talkin' about Austin with fellow Texans, you can discuss any crazy experiences you may have had while there, or even what random delicious foods you might have tried.

EXAMPLE CONVERSATION

FELLOW TEXAN: "Have you ever been to Austin?"

YOU: "Yes, actually I was just there. It was very random, but fun."

FELLOW TEXAN: "How so?"

YOU: "Well, I saw a guy ridin' a unicycle to work, and for lunch we ate chicken and waffle donuts."

FELLOW TEXAN: "That is weird."

YOU: "I know. Very weird."

THE BIPOLAR WEATHER

It don't matter where you live in the world, the weather is gonna change frequently. Texas is no different in that regard. What does seem to be different is the extremes to which it does so. On any given day it can swing from 70° and cloudy to 110° and dry. The seasons just don't count. You can have a Christmas day with shorts weather and still be sportin' a long-sleeve shirt much of the way into March.

This bein' the case, it's an easy thing to chitchat about with pretty much anyone. Us Texans just never seem to get tired of discussin' it with other folks. Go ahead and fire up one of these conversations and folks will think you've been here for generations.

EXAMPLE CONVERSATION

GROCERY STORE CLERK: "Hello, how're you doin' today?"

YOU: "I'm doin' fine, thank you. I'd be better though if this weather wasn't givin' me whiplash!"

GROCERY STORE CLERK: "I know! When I came outside this mornin' it was cold. Now I'm burnin' up!"

YOU: "I swear that storm moved through here faster than small-town gossip."

GROCERY STORE CLERK: "Yup"

YOU: "See ya later!"

GROCERY STORE CLERK: "Adios!"

MEANWHILE IN HOUSTON

THE TRAFFIC

Traffic is a problem regardless of where you live in Texas, but it comes in many different forms. In a big city like Houston or San Antonio, it could be caused by an accident and the rubberneckers that feel the need to gawk at the wreck. In a small town like Stonewall or Crystal City, it could be caused by a tractor that's takin' up one whole lane on a two-lane road.

With the distances between places in Texas bein' so large, it's no wonder that we're an impatient bunch. Take advantage of this impatience and discuss the inconveniences with your friends. The process of discussin' this shared experience will trick other Texans into thinkin' you're from around here, and it'll probably help lower your blood pressure the more you have to deal with it yourself.

EXAMPLE CONVERSATION

FELLOW TEXAN: "I can't believe how long it took to get here."

YOU: "I know! I was makin' good time until I got caught by the train that cuts through town."

FELLOW TEXAN: "Oh man, that's the worst! Happens to me every time I'm in a rush."

YOU: "This one was a long one, too. It slowed down to a crawl and prolly took twenty minutes to pass."

FELLOW TEXAN: "I wish they'd build a bridge over that railroad crossin'."

YOU: "You and me both."

Favorite BBQ Joints

"I'm gonna Instagram the brisket I ate earlier."
—Blanca, San Antonio

In the rest of the country, politics can be super divisive. It's not to say that they're not here as well. It's just that we've got more important things to debate, like which BBQ joints are the best. Every Texan fancies themselves as a BBQ expert, so it should come as no surprise that relationships have ended over disagreements about BBQ.

I can't tell you what to say in the event that you or someone else decides to start talkin' about BBQ, because it's all a matter of opinion. I would just recommend studyin' up on the BBQ knowledge presented in Chapter 6 so you at least know the basics. Not knowin' anything about BBQ is one of the fastest ways for a foreigner to get figured out by Texans. Not everyone in Texas can bar-b-que themselves, but everyone knows enough about the meats, sides, and process to hold their own at a dinner table or over a few beers. In fact, I'm pretty sure it's state law that people have a basic understandin'.

Favorite Tex-Mex Joints

This subject matter falls into the same realm as BBQ in that it's highly subjective to your tastes. Regardless of that, it's still an important area of knowledge for you to possess. There's some in-depth Tex-Mex'ducation provided in Chapter 6, but in the meantime figure out whether you prefer corn or flour tortillas and if you're a green salsa or red salsa kinda person. The rest you'll pick up as you go along, and when you do, you'll be ready to chat it up with anyone.

"Don't ask me. I wanted pizza."
—Miranda, Beaumont

HOW TO ENGAGE WITH FOREIGNERS

As time passes and you grow more comfortable with your newfound Texan status, the less palatable you will become to non-Texans. This is a normal byproduct of bein' Texan and you shouldn't be concerned about it. Those of us who grew up here grew accustomed to it at a young age. Luckily it doesn't take long for newcomers like yourself to acclimate either.

The hardest part about bein' Texan is dealing with all the jealousy that people who aren't from Texas have about Texas. Don't listen to what they say about how obnoxious you are, how overblown Texas's value is, or how backwards they think we are. At the end of the day, they're just jealous of what we've got. Honestly, if I lived in New Jersey or Florida, I'd be just as sour as they are too.

Treading lightly won't help you much when it comes to dealing with these folks, so playin' down your Texan traits when they're around isn't advised. If anything, I say you should swing for the bleachers and really lay it on thick. Any sign of weakness in your Texan pride will only serve to empower non-Texans into thinkin' that they are superior. They'll be led to believe that simply being put off by our charms will be enough for us to lessen those charms.

Instead of pullin' back on the reigns of your Texas pride, I'll give you some quick guidelines for things that non-Texans don't want to hear. Bein' the friendly Texan that you are, you can utilize it for the purposes of not pissin' anyone off. Just remember that doing' so is your choice and not a product of any highfalutin Yankee's displeasure with your demeanor. If you want to go 100 percent full Texan on them, do it 'til the cows come home.

Don't talk about how much better Texas is than where they are from.

It's not kind to kick a person when they're down. Although they're not down from takin' a beatin', they do have the unfortunate luck of bein' from somewhere that just ain't Texas. This is a pretty horrible situation to be in. Be the bigger person and leave their home out of it.

 Don't talk about how bad their food tastes compared to ours.

Believe me. I've eaten food from outside of Texas and as far as I'm concerned there's nothin' cuisine about the cuisine I've eaten. I'll tell you what . . . it's glorified slop. Regardless of this fact, it's still considered uncouth to trash someone else's cookin'.

 Don't talk about how much bigger Texas is than everywhere else.

It don't matter where you go. When you bring this fact up, there's always some self-appointed geography expert who likes to remind Texans that Alaska is in fact much larger than Texas. What that person always seems to forget is the fact that there are probably more people livin' on Mars than there are in Alaska. Bears, salmon, and Alaskan king crab don't count towards the population.

 Don't talk about how unfriendly the people are from places other than Texas.

Between you and I, they're horrible. They don't care about how anyone else is doin'. They don't hold doors open for one another. They don't care to chat with strangers. It's just plain awful. I couldn't agree with you more on this point. Despite that, bite your tongue and keep it to yourself. I know us Texans are emotional people and it's hard to hide what we're thinkin', but there's no faster way to piss off a non-Texan than to tell 'em how rude they are. Believe me.

 Don't talk about how much smaller and cute their cars are.

Texans drive bigger cars and trucks because they're the only vehicles large enough to haul around our Texas pride. Being reminded that their cars are tiny by comparison will only serve to make them feel inadequate. Just don't broach the subject with them.

 Don't talk about how we were once our own country.

It's difficult to decipher why exactly this is the case, but non-Texans don't like hearin' about our previous republic. I'm not sure if they're afraid that we could secede and survive without them (we could) or if they're just annoyed with the idea of havin' to get a passport to visit Texas (I would be), but it just seems to get under their skin. Let it alone and let the fact that we're basically a country that's undercover as a state sustain you.

 Don't talk about how we do things in Texas.

As backwards as it is for someone to call grillin' hot dogs and hamburgers BBQ, tellin' someone that they're wrong won't do much for helping the cause. It's better to lead by example in these instances. Invite these poor lost souls to visit us in Texas and show them the way. They'll be way more responsive than if you tell them they're wrong.

 Don't talk about how the state of Texas has always weathered nationwide economic hardships like a boss.

With a few exceptions that we won't discuss here, Texas has generally been an economic powerhouse. Like we said before, it ain't kind to kick a person when they're down. Discussin' how well we're doin' financially with a group of folks who ain't doin' quite as well is just plain rude. It's okay to be proud of the economy we've built and the boats and trucks we've bought. It's just not nice to talk about with strangers. Especially broke strangers.

DRESSIN' TEXAN

Sample Material:

TEXAS STEREOTYPES • COWBOY HATS

COWBOY BOOTS • OPTIONAL ACCESSORIES

Texans for the most part have never learned how to be dull.

—Randolph B. Campbell

Texas doesn't have a dress code per se. The beauty of livin' here is our appreciation for individuality and self-expression. Granted, all the weird folk may congregate in Austin, but that's by their own choice and not by any forced wrangling of folks done by the rest of us.

All that bein' said, whether you're more of an Austin Texan or an Everywhere Else Texan, you're free to dress however you'd like. Although the Texan mystique is heavily based on cowboys and all-around Western awesomeness, we've got plenty of folks who aren't cattle ranchers or rodeo cowboys. Feel free to settle into whatever kinda clothes you feel most comfortable in.

Get off my property!

Classy!

REDNECK
- Camo clothing
- They'll spot you before you spot them
- Shoots first, asks questions later

SOCIALITE
- Wears expensive clothing
- Probably from Dallas
- Does not like mud

US TEXANS LOVE BROAD GENERALIZATIONS, SO HERE ARE SOME STEREOTYPES FOR YOU TO SHARPEN YOUR STEREOTYPIN' SKILLS WITH.

Let's go two-step!

Over my dead body!

DANCE HALL ANGEL
- Wears summer dress with boots
- Loves to two-step
- Known to steal the hearts of many men

GUN ENTHUSIAST
- Wears firearms as clothing accessory
- Has A LOT of guns
- Understands gun laws better than most lawyers

COWBOY

- Wears hat, starched jeans, and boots
- Spurs are optional
- Lassos pretty much everything in sight
- Rides horse everywhere

Is this dress gluten free?

AUSTIN HIPPIE

- Wears hippie stuff
- Likes to keep things weird
- Eats primarily vegetables
- Just wants world peace and to play hacky sack

Yeehaw!

COWGIRL

- Wears hat, jeans, and boots
- Jewelry optional
- Can drink you under the table
- Not to be messed with

Siri, where is the nearest gastropub?

HIPSTER GUY

- Grows beard as accessory
- Thick-rimmed glasses
- Eats a lot of artisanal things, whatever that means

Lookin' to Reinvent Yourself?

A lot of folks find their way to Texas because they weren't happy with where they lived, or who they were when they lived elsewhere. It's understandable. And really, can you blame 'em? Everywhere that Ain't Texas sucks.

Let's just say for argument's sake that you're one of those individuals. If you're already gonna be startin' with a clean slate anyway, why not cowboy up and go full Texan from the start? It's not terribly difficult.

The benefits of becomin' a walkin', talkin' Texas cliché are too numerous to list here, but I assure you that they're amazing, so dive in.

"Pretending to own a ranch got a hell of a lot easier once I moved to Texas. It's the full Texan that really sells it."

—Rick,
formerly of Florida

" I was a regional sales manager, wearing pantsuits everyday. Now look at me!"

—Tina, formerly of Arizona

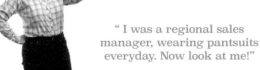

"We used to hate our parents until we moved to Texas and they let us dress like this."

—Braden and Jared,
formerly of Missouri

COWBOY HATS

Now that you've decided to let us redo ya, we'll start from the top with the hat. Cowboy hats and Texas go hand in hand. Everyone should own at least one. They can be quite the over-whelming purchase to make, though, so I'm gonna walk you through the basics.

Cowboy Hat

This is a cowboy hat. It serves the purpose of keepin' the sun off your head and face, warms your head in the winter, and frankly just looks cool.

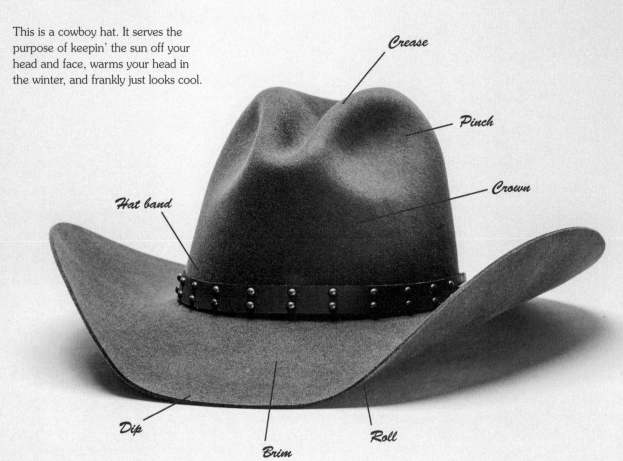

Crease

Pinch

Crown

Hat band

Dip

Brim

Roll

HAT MATERIAL

The two main types of material used in cowboy hat makin' are fur-based felt and straw. Felt hats will keep your head warmer in the winter, but don't breathe quite as well and are heavier than straw. Straw, on the other hand, makes for a lighter and less-formal-lookin' hat, so it can't be dressed up as easily as a felt one can—though George Strait could make either look sharp. It's all a matter of preference and style, though, so that decision-makin' is up to you.

Oftentimes you'll see a series of "X"s on the sweatband on the inside of the brim. The more "X"s you see, the higher the quality of the materials being used in the production of the hat. As with most things, as that increases, so does the cost. Don't feel the need to blow through cash and buy a 10X hat on your first at bat. Just get one that feels right for you.

Straw on straw

The weathered look, in felt

CROWN

The crown of a cowboy hat is the tall portion in the middle that sits directly above your head. The style of crown you choose for yourself is also a matter of personal preference, but to give you an idea of the many variations, take a look at the illustrations below.

CATTLEMAN

OPEN

PINCHED FRONT

GUS CROWN

PUNCHER

BRICK

GAMBLER

EXTRA WIDE

POINTED

ROUND

BRIM

SQUARE

WIDE

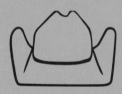

Finally, you need to select a brim length and style. The general rule of thumb is that you want the brim to be roughly the width of your shoulders. Personally I've got a skinny face, so wide-brim hats look a little outta place on me. Above are basic brim styles. Most brims can be reshaped to whatever style you prefer.

Cowboy Boots

Hats may be hard for all folks, includin' yourself, to wear all the time. Face it, we don't all work on ranches anymore. Don't fret, though. You can still keep the cowboy spirit alive with a nice pair of boots. As with the cowboy hat, there are a lot of options to consider, so don't get overwhelmed. Here's one of my old boots to get you accustomed to their parts.

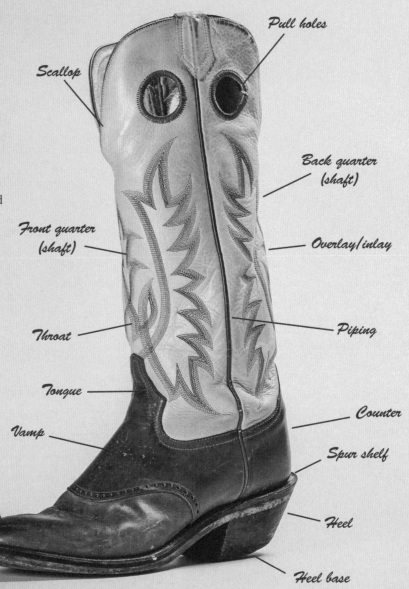

Pull holes

Scallop

Back quarter
(shaft)

Front quarter
(shaft)

Overlay/inlay

Throat

Piping

Tongue

Vamp

Counter

Spur shelf

Toe box

Outsole

Heel

Heel base

BOOT STYLES

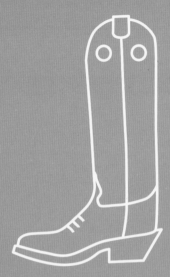

BUCKAROO

If you're lookin' to make a statement, the buckaroo-style boot is the way to go. It's tall, decorated, and full of Western punch. Some people say it ain't practical for everyday wear. Ignore those people.

COWBOY

The classic cowboy boot is one part functional and one part punch. It's comfortable for walkin' and stylish enough to be acceptable at weddings, dinner, or a bar.

ROPER

The roper-style boot has a lower, wider heel that is perfect for workin' in. It's the most comfortable of the styles, so if you plan on doin' any manual work in Texas, you'll want to pick up a pair.

PLACES WHERE COWBOY BOOTS ARE ACCEPTABLE FOOTWEAR

Churches
Weddings
Business meetings
Ridin' in your truck
The gun range
While jogging
Your own funeral
Dancing
New York (not that you'd go)
While skateboarding

FREQUENTLY ASKED BOOT QUESTIONS

"Do I have to take off my boots when I go inside a house?"
If it's your momma's house, unless you're God or George Strait, you'd better take those boots off before you go in.

"I'm a guy who likes shorts. Can I wear boots with them?"
No.

"I love my cowboy boots!"
That's great, but that's not a question.

TOE

Depending on the shape of your feet and length of your toes, the toe of the boot can be of great importance, not only for style, but also for comfort. Some offer more room for your toes to roam than others. If you're lookin' for a particular style, it's important as well.

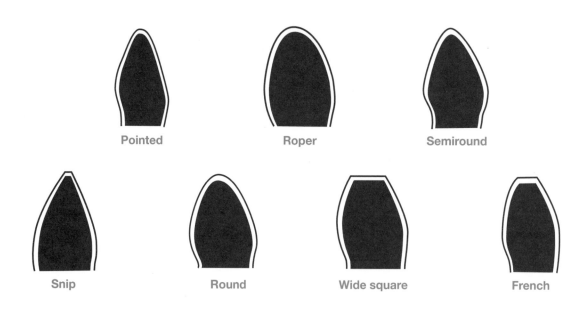

Pointed   Roper   Semiround

Snip   Round   Wide square   French

SCALLOP

Double rose   Extra deep   Deep   Shallow   Stovepipe

HEEL

The heel of the cowboy boot adds a lot to the overall look. Women are used to wearin' taller heels, but for men it may come as a big change from what they're used to. Luckily, you've got options for both men's and women's boots between taller heels and short, flat-footed boots. Go tall for the "punchy" look and go short for the comfortable, everyday walkin' heel.

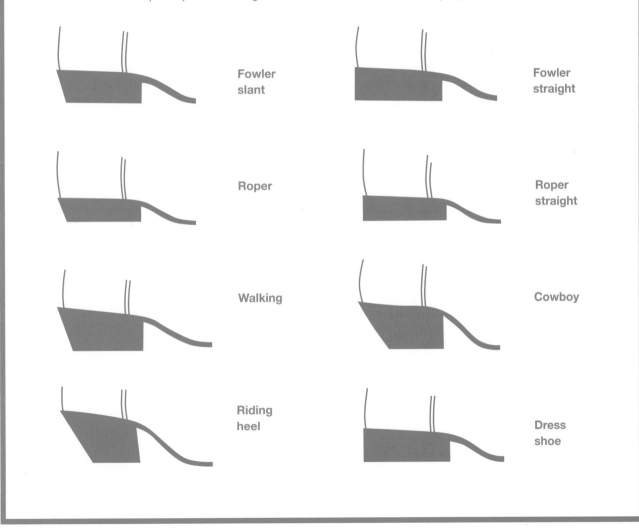

Fowler slant

Fowler straight

Roper

Roper straight

Walking

Cowboy

Riding heel

Dress shoe

BOOT MATERIAL

IF TEXANS CAN BBQ ANYTHING, YOU'D BETTER BELIEVE THAT WE CAN MAKE BOOTS OUT OF ANYTHING. COW, ALLIGATOR, OSTRICH, GOAT, AND MANY OTHERS ARE ALL OPTIONS WHEN CHOOSING. OF COURSE, PRICES CHANGE WITH EVERY ANIMAL, AND YOUR MILEAGE MAY VARY WITH REGARD TO COMFORT. THIS IS MY TAKE ON WHAT WOULD AND WOULDN'T MAKE FOR A GOOD PAIR OF BOOTS. BEING A TEXAN, I'M NOT ONE TO SAY SOMETHING CAN'T BE DONE, SO FEEL FREE TO TRY WHATEVER YOU'D LIKE.

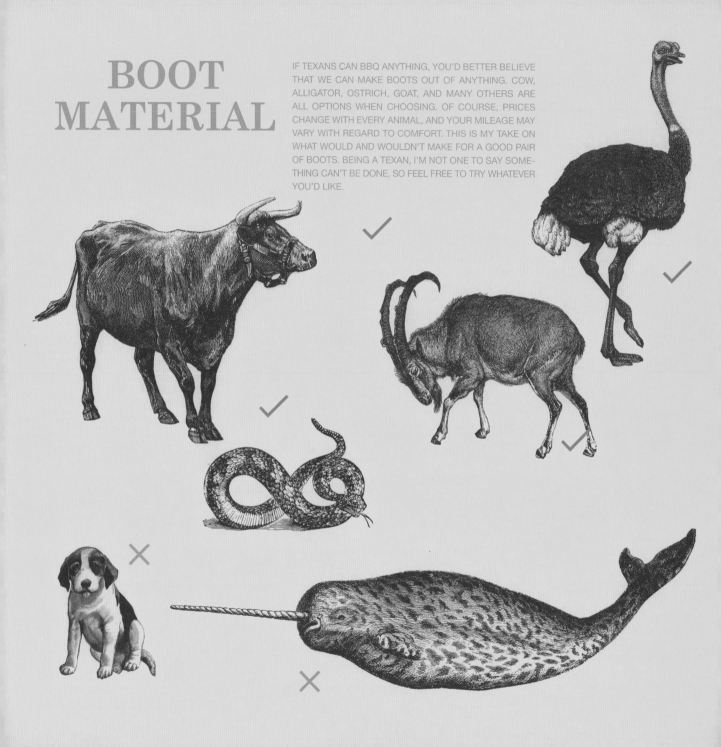

COWBOY
VEST

"AIN'T TEXAS"
SHIRT

TEXAS FLAG
DRESS SHIRT

TEXAS FLAG
BIKINI

OPTIONAL ACCESSORIES

There are a lot of things a budding Texan like yourself can wear to help solidify your newborn identity. In addition to what we've already covered, grab a few of these accessories to really jazz up that new stereotypical-Texan you.

TEXAS FLAG
NECKLACE

TEXAS
TATTOO

HOLSTER AND GUN
(NOW THAT OPEN
CARRY PASSED)

TEXAS DPS-STYLE
SUNGLASSES

"Dressin' Texan makes me
feel like a spring chicken."
—Juan, San Benito

"My hat increases my
Texan-ness 150 percent."
—Les, Carrizo Springs

5

TEXAN TRADITIONS

Sample Material:

FOOTBALL • PEP RALLIES • HOMECOMING • MUMS • RODEO

THE STATE FAIR • FRYIN' • BIG TEX

The influence that football has on Texan culture cannot be overstated. Texas only has two seasons: football season and not football season. It's a sport that was developed in the Northeast, but perfected in Texas. Your understanding of its role in our lives is crucial to your bein' considered a real Texan. As an amateur sport, it is played in backyards amongst family and friends. On a professional level, it generates millions of dollars of revenue each year. Whether you have any desire to play the sport yourself or not, I assure you it's gonna play a big part of your life year-round.

FOOTBALL IS TO TEXAS WHAT RELIGION IS TO A PRIEST.

—TOM LANDRY

" FOOTBALL IS COOLER THAN CHURCH! *"*

—MARK, 8

" IT'S THE ONLY THING MY SON AND I HAVE TO TALK ABOUT. *"*

—BOB, 63

" I CAN'T STAND MY WIFE, BUT I LOVE WATCHING FOOTBALL. *"*

—RICHARD, 37

" I HATE SOCCER. *"*

—PAM, 52

Ye ol' pigskin

The Basics

I'm not certain what the sports are that you played wherever it is that you're from. Whatever they were, just keep 'em to yourself. Football is kinda like rugby, but with less British people, and a lot fewer long-sleeve striped shirts. It's like that soccer game that the rest of the world cares so much about, only it's exciting and more fun to watch. It's like baseball, except no one makes you stand up and sing "Take Me Out to the Football Stadium" three-quarters of the way through the game.

Goin' to a football game in Texas is like seein' a gladiator match at the Colosseum during the height of the Roman Empire. It's pure spectacle and action, but when it's over no one gets fed to a lion. The only real lasting physical harm is the damage to the egos of the losin' team.

How do you play, you ask? Well here's a fast and dirty explanation. Two teams of eleven players play on a long rectangular field with goalposts at each end. They fight for control of an oval-shaped ball, which they try to move to the opposite end of the field. We like to call this ball a pigskin.

Anyway, the offense, which is the team that currently has the ball, will try to move the ball downfield by throwin' it or runnin' it along the field. The defense, also known as the team that doesn't currently have the ball, will try to prevent them from doin' that, all while tryin' to steal the ball for themselves.

You score points by gettin' the ball to the other end of the field that the defense is defendin'. You can get some extra points by kickin' the ball through the goalposts that are at the end of the field as well.

There are slight variations of the rules depending on if it's high school, college, or professional league play; and depending on the region or number of people available to play, the teams may vary in size.

For now, though, since we're mainly focused on teachin' you how to be the best Texan you can be, we'll walk through the culture that surrounds the sport.

Protectin' ye ol' melon

TEXAS HIGH SCHOOL FOOTBALL BASICS

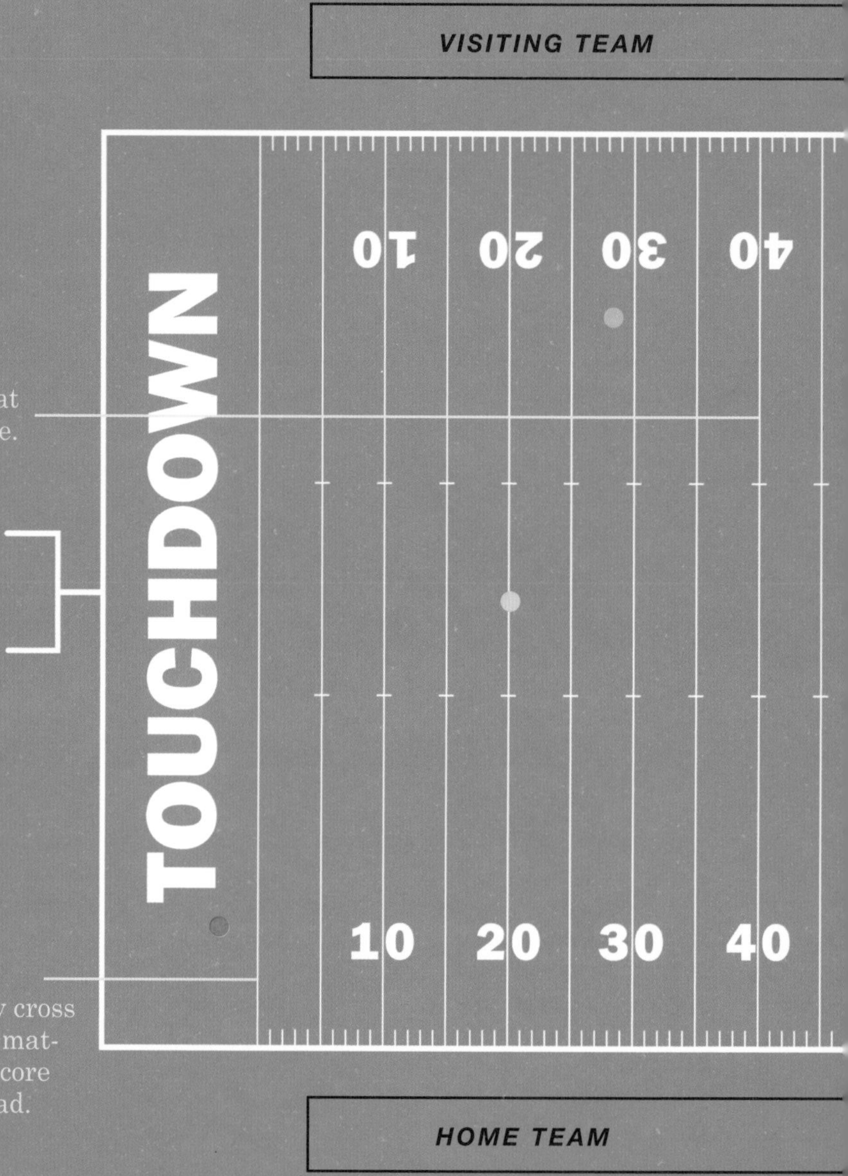
VISITING TEAM
10
20
30
40
TOUCHDOWN
10
20
30
40
HOME TEAM

Kickoff happens at the forty yard line.

Six points for the other jerks if they cross this line. Doesn't matter; even if they score they still can't read.

Six points for your team when the ball crosses this line. Then you have to hope your kicker doesn't miss the extra point.

VISITING TEAM

40 30 20 10

TOUCHDOWN

40 30 20 10

HOME TEAM

FAMOUS SPOTS ON THE LOCAL GRIDIRON

- 1989: Li'l Jared Donley, a ninth grader, was hit so hard that town folk still ask if he's okay.

- 1995: Brad Marshall catches pass to win state title, making him a local legend. Free beers and handshakes forever.

- 2004: Senior Stu Taylor tackled while streaking. Cops said he cried the entire way to jail.

- 2005: Brian Hyde ejected for throwing wild kidney punch at unsuspecting lineman.

- 2008: Sophomore Shaun Lind realizes he's scored a touchdown for the wrong team.

- 2014: On first day of practice, freshman Barrett Fry realizes he's trying out for the wrong "football." He immediately regrets trying to throw in front of other teammates.

HIGH SCHOOL FOOTBALL

Pretty much every town in Texas has a high school, which means pretty much every town in Texas has a football team. Knowin' that Texans are rabidly passionate and prideful, it should come as no surprise that this translates to friendly yet passionate competitions between cities.

It's easy to tell when football season starts in Texas. When football season is in full swing, it's not abnormal to see caravans of school buses, box trucks, and a slew of pickups and SUVs cruisin' down the highway with a police escort.

Don't be alarmed by this sight. A crazed high school math teacher did not kidnap a school bus full of children and lead their city on a wild police chase. What you're seein' is the holy ritual of one school travelin' to another school's stadium for a game. What is being transported inside those vehicles is what makes the tradition of Friday night football games so dang great. More on this later.

Coach
Slightly tubby-looking person. Whistle, baseball cap, shorts, and mustache.

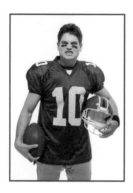

Football player
Normally relatively fit person, rolled-up jersey sleeves, holding helmet under arm. Joke about them dating the head cheerleader.

Band member
With big goofy-looking hat, holding a trumpet, sheet music.

Parents
Slightly overweight-ish dad with football team booster club shirt, visor, and sneakers, holding a padded folding seat back for bleachers. Mom wearing shorts and a high school T-shirt as well.

Cheerleader
Propensity to ask large crowds to spell things. Must be bossy enough to yell at crowds and tell them to do things. Guy cheerleaders must be strong enough to throw the girls up in the air.

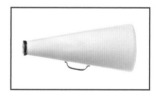

Props
Megaphone, pom-poms, painted signs.

Pep Rallies

Before we even start puttin' kids on school buses and haulin' them down state highways, it all starts with a pep rally. This spectacle is normally held in a high school gymnasium. Normally the high school's marchin' band drumline will lead the school to the gym, where the principal, a few coaches, and a couple of awkward football team members will say a few words about how good they are, etc. The band will play a song while the cheerleaders lead some cheers to get everyone pumped up for the game that night. Sprinkled in are generally some antics involving the school mascot as well.

BEFORE THE GAME

A couple of hours before the game, the parking lot of the home team will start to fill up with students and parents who help keep things running smoothly at the stadium. Moms and dads will normally help run the ticket booth, and volunteer organizations sell the nachos, hot dogs, and cokes you'll snack on at the concession stand. Being that this is Texas and we do everything to the max, nowadays some of the high school stadiums even have Jumbotrons that are normally run by the kids from the AV class.

Mascots

Parents

**Cool kids
that don't
play sports**

Instruments

**Police
escort**

THE
FOOTBALL
MOTORCADE

As I alluded to earlier, football is serious business in Texas. A lot of small towns don't have that much goin' on, so it's not out of the ordinary for the local police to escort the students from the visiting school to the game. They stop traffic at intersections and give the team, marching band, and cheerleaders the same kind of priority afforded to heads of state.

**Drill
team**

The team

**Marching
band**

Cheerleaders

**Doctors /
physical therapist**

THE GAME ITSELF

The game begins just like any other football game. A referee flips a coin and things get under way. Competition is fierce because Texans are just better at football. Regardless of skill level, almost all the kids have hopes of being spotted by a scout and bein' asked to play football for one of Texas's many great universities.

So many games are takin' place at the same time on Friday nights, it's normal for the local news to spend a significant amount of time calling out all of the surrounding area's final scores. It's important information that all Texans need to know.

The coin flip: There are strong feelings over which side of the coin to choose. Some say heads, others tails. Both sides blame the other when the team loses.

HALFTIME

Halftime is a production all in itself. The drill team and marchin' bands aren't relegated to the sidelines the entire time. For the thirty minutes between play that is allocated to halftime, these students shine.

The marchin' band will normally cover some pop song or movie theme, all the while marchin' around the field and, with varying success, making letters that spell things out or shapes that reference the music that is currently bein' played.

Immediately afterwards, the drill team files out onto the field and does a dance number timed to some sort of high-energy pop music.

While this is all goin' on, proud parents cheer from the stands and utilize the handheld video cameras they bought for these exact events. It's a well-oiled machine in which every person knows their role.

The band, jammin'.

HOMECOMING

Once a year, a special game called the homecoming game is held. If you were to attend one of these games without bein' forewarned, I'm confident that you would be completely baffled by what you saw.

For one, each school normally tries to schedule their homecoming game the same week that they're playing someone who they deem "less than competitive." Ya see, homecoming is exactly for the purpose after which it was named. It's the one weekend that alumni are generally supposed to come home and attend a game. Ideally, everyone would love for this to happen when the home team is puttin' a Texas-sized whoopin' on some neighboring city's team. More often than not, it turns into a metaphorical bloodbath on the field, with the visiting team eventually leaving with their tail between their legs.

The second thing that would stick out would be the bizarre way students seem to be dressed for a football game. Young men are dressed in khakis and button-down shirts, while the young girls are wearing fancy dresses. On the young men's arms are little armbands with ribbons and bells hanging off, and on the young girls, massive versions of the decorations the boys are wearing. What are these things you ask? Well, funny you should ask.

HOMECOMING MUMS AND GARTERS

These large, wearable, fake flower gardens are known as homecoming mums. They're a tradition that's about as Texan as it gets. Their origin is based on the simple act of a young man givin' his homecoming dance date a flower. Over time, being Texans and all, we made the simple act of givin' a flower into a much more elaborate and fun tradition.

Along with the homecoming game, there is normally a homecoming dance that is held on Saturday night for the high schoolers to attend. Boys will ask girls to attend as their dates.

Rather than simply giving a flower, the tradition has developed into havin' larger and larger corsage-like arrangements built. They've grown to include things like stuffed animals and flashin' lights. They're real feats of engineerin'.

Don't mistake the DIY-lookin' nature of these things to mean they're cheap, either. A big ol' back-breakin' mum will set a kid back a couple hundred bucks in some parts.

The flower wearin' isn't limited to the ladies, either. Most girls give their dates what amounts to a miniature version of their mum, known as a garter. The garter is equally as loud, but is worn on the bicep of the fella the nights of the football game and dance.

The smaller sibling of the homecoming mum is the homecoming garter. It ain't big, but it's still loud.

MUM ANATOMY

In most cases, homecoming mums are decorated with trinkets and materials that reference the colors of the wearer's high school. In our example below, we turned the Texan up to eleven and built it for the fictional Texas High School. Your mileage may vary.

Texas flag

I'm of the humble opinion that all mums should be topped with a Texas flag, but that's just me.

Fake bluebonnet

Homecoming happens in the fall, which ain't prime bluebonnet season, so a fake'll have to do.

Tiny cowboy hat

You can't get much more Texan than a cowboy hat.

Chili pepper

Let your gal know you think she's hot by addin' little chili peppers to her mum.

Koozie

What is a Texan if not prepared for anything? Dangle a koozie on there and she'll be prepared for any beverage that's thrown her way.

Stuffed armadillo

The centerpiece of a mum is generally a stuffed animal. What better animal than the Texas speed bump, aka the armadillo?

Fake flowers

A mum ain't a mum if it ain't got fake flowers for the base. In this case we went full Texan and used 'em to make an outline of the state of Texas.

Fluffy boa

A bit of fluff really accentuates that Texas border.

Whataburger stickers

Whataburger "special" stickers let her know she's not just anyone. She's "special."

Streamers

The more the merrier. Just don't make 'em so long your date will trip on 'em.

Tiny cowbell

There's bein' loud visually and then there's bein' loud literally. Let 'em know you're comin' before you do.

RODEO

The rodeo is about as Texan as you can get in terms of traditions. Born out of the tasks and skills needed for cattle ranchin', the rodeo is a competitive event that mixes one part ego with one part crazy and several parts on'ry livestock.

In Texas, you can attend rodeos of all sizes. You've got your small local rodeos with a handful of participants all the way up to the largest rodeo around held in Houston in the spring. The Houston Livestock Show and Rodeo is as big as all get out.

GRAND ENTRY

Most rodeos start with a big display of riders on horseback and sometimes wagons traveling around the rodeo ring and eventually standing attention in the center while holdin' up Texas and American flags. The entry is often used to introduce everyone to the participants (as well as the sponsors).

HORSEBACK EVENTS

Rodeo events vary from one rodeo to another, but most will include some form of what's called ropin', which is exactly what it sounds like. In team ropin', two folks on horseback chase down a steer. One, "the header," lassos the steer's horns, while the other, "the heeler," ropes the steer's hind legs till they pull the steer over to the ground. There's a singles version of this event as well where a cowboy (or cowgirl for that

matter) chases a calf down on horseback, lassos it around the neck, then "coaxes" it to the ground and finally ties up three of its legs as quickly as possible.

Of course, bein' that horses are just plain fun to ride, barrel racing is another type of horseback event that simply involves runnin' your horse as fast as you can around a series of barrels in a cloverleaf pattern without knockin' any of them over.

Bulls: Large, and generally not willing to let you sit on their backs. Google "Bull Riding Wrecks" if you want more info.

ROUGH STOCK EVENTS

The events everybody loves watchin' are what are known as the rough stock events. These events involve cowboys ridin' on the back of horses and bulls that just plain don't like for them to be there. Bull ridin' is exactly what it sounds like it is. A brave cowboy hops on the back of a pissed off bull and tries to stay on it with one hand for at least eight seconds. Bronc ridin' is the same type of deal, except with a madder than hell horse.

RODEO CLOWNS

When a cowboy falls off a bull after it's just spent the last eight seconds pissin' it off, said bull ain't gonna be the happiest of participants. The role of drawing the bull away from the cowboy who is currently trying to pick themselves up outta the mud, falls to the rodeo clown. These clowns aren't solely of the laughter incitin' type. They are tough folks who draw the bulls away from others in the bull ridin' ring as well as provide comic relief to the audience in attendance.

MUTTON BUSTIN'

One of my favorite events at many modern rodeos is the mutton bustin', in large part due to its sheer hilariousness. The idea behind mutton bustin' is similar to bronco ridin', except instead of a bull, we use a sheep, and instead of a cowboy, we use children under about fifty pounds. It's pretty safe and highly entertaining. The kiddos wear a helmet and protective vest, and are lowered onto a sheep that then takes off runnin' into the rodeo ring. The kiddo then tries to hold on for dear life as long as possible. Believe me when I say it's hilarious and pretty much harmless. The only thing that gets injured is a few kiddos' pride.

TEXAS-OKLAHOMA RIVALRY

When folks in Texas talk about football rivalries, the University of Texas versus Texas A&M is the big one that comes to mind. But the University of Texas and University of Oklahoma football rivalry is equally large, due to the pitting of the state of Texas versus its jealous and less-attractive little sibling, Oklahoma.

The rivalry takes place yearly in the Cotton Bowl, which is located in the center of the state fairgrounds. On the weekend that this game is held, thousands of Texans hop in their trucks and haul butt up to Dallas to partake in the festivities. It's a highly contentious game and one that I highly recommend you experience.

THE STATE FAIR

The State Fair of Texas is one of the greatest traditions you'll get to experience as a Texan. Held every year since 1886 (with the exception of some lapses durin' the world wars), it's located at the Fair Park in Dallas, Texas. The fair runs for roughly a month, starting at the end of September and continuing on through October. Modeled after world's fairs, the state fair is an exhibition of some of the greatest things about Texas.

Get yourself a couple of corny dogs. Wash down with ⟶

After the beers, maybe try your hand at a few games. Not the bottle one though. That one's hard and you'll probably leave embarrassed.

FRYIN' OLYMPICS

One of the best things about our state is the food, and one area that we excel in is fryin' things. Food at fairs is rarely of the snooty type, so it's to be expected that you'll only find fried foods at any fair you go to. What isn't necessarily expected is a menu that includes fried butter, fried Oreos, or fried Snickers.

Below is a list of real things that have been fried and sold for human consumption over the years. Bear in mind that none of these are made up and all are totally possible. When there's a will, there's a way.

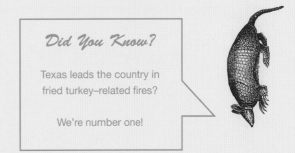

REESE'S PEANUT BUTTER CUPS • **BEER** (yes, it's possible—"impossible" is not a word Texans understand)

PECAN PIE • **FRITO PIE** • **KING RANCH CASSEROLE** • **CHEESECAKE**

JAMBALAYA • **SPAGHETTI AND MEATBALLS** • **GRILLED CHEESE SANDWICH**

SWEET TEA • **SMOKED BRISKET** • **LATTE** • **MILK AND COOKIES** • **AVOCADO**

PB&J BANANA SANDWICH • **LOADED BAKED POTATOES** • **TEXAS BLUEBONNET (BLUEBERRY MUFFIN)**

SRIRACHA BALLS • **GULF SHRIMP BOIL** • **PORK RIND NACHOS** • **BUBBLEGUM**

COCA-COLA • **BACON (OF COURSE)** • **JELLY BEANS** • **CADBURY CREME EGGS**

KOOL-AID • **SALSA** • **POP-TARTS** • **MARGARITA**

CLUB SALAD (leave it to a Texan to make a salad unhealthy)

S'MORES • **BACON CINNAMON ROLL**

TEXAS STAR FERRIS WHEEL

Close to the midway games section of the State Fair you'll find the tallest Ferris wheel in the United States (of course it is). On your next visit, I highly recommend buyin' some ride tickets and takin' a ride in one of the forty-five gondolas. You'll get great views of the city of Dallas as well as the fella we're about to talk about next.

All this talk about the fair and we've glossed over one of the biggest attractions: Big Tex. He's a fifty-five-foot-tall Texan at the center of the park who welcomes guests with a mighty "Howdy, folks" throughout the entire festival. Since 1952 he's been keepin' watch of the fair while wearin' a giant pair of boots, jeans, and western-cut shirt.

BIG TEX BURNS

In 2012, the year of Big Tex's sixtieth birthday, tragedy struck when a fire engulfed Big Tex, destroyin' his head, hat, and clothes. In true Texan fashion and unfazed by this short-term setback, the powers that be rebuilt Big Tex taller and heavier to withstand stronger winds (likely due to all the hot air Texans are filled with). In 2013 he was back in the saddle welcomin' folks young and old back to the fair. You just can't keep a good Texan down, no matter how big or small.

EATIN' TEXAN

Sample Material:

THE TEXAS FOOD PYRAMID • HOW TO CORRECTLY SNACK • TEX-MEX

TACOS • CHILI • BAR-B-QUE • SIDES AND BEVERAGES

THE MEATS • WILD GAME

It's been said that Texas is a place where they barbecue everything except ice cream.

—Rosemary Kent

Eatin' correctly is an important part of being a Texan. I'm not referrin' to a balanced diet or anything like that. It's all about eatin' the correct things and eatin' a lot of it. I'm not here to suggest that overeatin' is a good thing for your health at all. All I'm suggestin' is that if you're gonna be a Texan, you might as well enjoy all the wonderful foods we have in Texas.

I hope you're hungry, because you're about to learn about the best that Texas cookin' has to offer, includin' a couple of my favorite recipes.

THE TEXAS FOOD PYRAMID

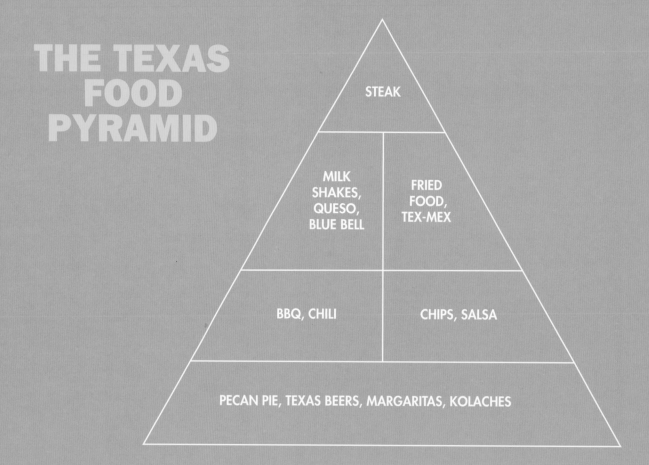

STEAK

MILK SHAKES, QUESO, BLUE BELL

FRIED FOOD, TEX-MEX

BBQ, CHILI

CHIPS, SALSA

PECAN PIE, TEXAS BEERS, MARGARITAS, KOLACHES

If you're wonderin' how to keep in shape while livin' in Texas, the Texas diet is the way to go. It's not that it'll help you lose weight. In fact, it's not likely to help you do that at all. Quite the opposite actually. "In shape" is a relative term. The food here will get you in a shape. It just might not be the shape you've got in mind.

All that bein' said, Texas is a diverse place with a lot of diverse ideas. About the only thing we all agree on is that the food in Texas is the best there is anywhere. Now that you understand that concept, let's get to eatin'.

THE TEXAS BACHELOR PYRAMID

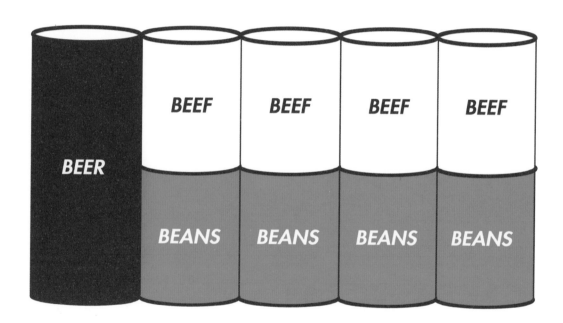

PECANS

To clarify for you Northerners, in Texas it's pronounced *puh-cahn'*, not pee'-can. You're probably familiar with this all-time Texas-favorite. We love crackin' 'em and eatin' the meat straight up, or makin' all kinds of baked goods (which we'll elaborate on later).

HOW TO CORRECTLY SNACK

SNACKIN' IN TEXAS IS ONE OF OUR NATIONAL PASTIMES, AND IT'S THE PLACE WE'LL START ON THIS JOURNEY THROUGH THE TEXAS DIET. SOME OF THESE SNACKS ARE REGIONAL DELIGHTS, BUT THEY'RE ALL VERY TEXAN NONETHELESS.

PICKLES

You might be thinkin' to yourself, What is so Texan about pickles? We have them where I come from. You'd be right for thinkin' that. We didn't invent pickles, but we sure as heck love snackin' on them. They're perfect for baseball games, sittin' on the porch, or takin' their juice and usin' it as flavor for ...

SNOW CONES/RASPAS

For children (and adults), one of the best tools for combating the Texas heat is a good old-fashioned snow cone. Shaved ice, or sno-balls, as the folks from Louisiana like to call them, are cool, fun, and cheap as all get-out. The flavors are endless, and a popular one, especially down south, is one flavored with pickle juice. My wife loves gettin' her snow cones pickadilly style, which means toppin' whatever your flavor of choice is with tiny bits of chopped pickle. (I told you we like pickles.)

CHIPS

and

SALSA

I have never met a single Texan who does not like chips and salsa. The chips I'm referrin' to are not the Lay's or SunChips you ate back in California or New York. These are tortilla chips, which you may or may not have had. They're paired with an amazing blend of tomatoes, cilantro, jalapeño peppers, garlic, and various other spices that when combined form this thing called salsa.

Like Lay's potato chips, you can't eat just one. When faced with a bowl of chips and a bowl of red or green salsa, you'll eat until you're not hungry for anything else. It's considered a snack, but it's also an appetite killer, which is a significant problem considerin' it's given away for free at the establishments that serve the food we're gonna chat about in the next section.

ANYTHING TEXAS SHAPED

Everything from Texas is better. Period. Everything shaped like Texas tastes better. It's science. When shoppin' at your local Texas grocery store, you may be surprised to find so many products shaped like our great state. Bring a few of these edible Texases back to your casa (Spanish for "home") and enjoy.

ICE CREAM

There's a little creamery down in Brenham, Texas, that has been churnin' out the best homemade-style ice cream for years and years, and us Texans are big fans. Texans not bein' the type to limit ourselves, Blue Bell doesn't just stick to ice cream. They produce popsicles, ice cream sandwiches, and a slew of other products that all help make summertime enjoyable. Travel to many a general store around the state and inside there'll be a big sign signifyin' hand-scooped ice cream cones featurin' the best little creamery in Texas.

BEEF JERKY

Jerky is the ubiquitous snack of the Texan tribe. Made by dryin' out beef cuts into tough yet tasty strips, you'll find it perfect for chompin' on year-round. Take a stroll down to any convenience store in Texas and you'll find more brands of jerky than you can shake a stick at. On top of the countless brands you'll find on the shelves, there are about six million (give or take a few million) different varieties. Teriyaki, black pepper, Texas BBQ style, hot, mild, you name it. My biggest recommendation when it comes to this stuff is to invest in good toothpicks, 'cause this'll end up stuck between every tooth you've got left in your head.

MEXICAN FRUIT CUP

Speakin' of bein' down south . . . Mexican fruit cups are all the rage and quite good, too. They're pretty much just cups of freshly sliced mixed fruit piled high in a Styrofoam cup with a bit of chili powder sprinkled on top. They're the perfect blend of spicy and sweet.

TEX-MEX

One of the greatest things to ever come out of the fusion of Texan and Tejano/Mexican cultures is the food. It's the perfect blend of shredded cheeses, beef, pork, beans, and spices. Not only is it delicious, it's cheap, makin' it all the more dangerous to the waistline.

The basis of all good Tex-Mex meals is some combination of rice (or as they say in Spanish, *arroz*), beans (*frijoles*), and tortillas (*tortillas*).

The rice is a simple dish you'd recognize like any other rice dish, normally flavored with tomato bouillon, cumin, and cilantro. The best beans are generally pinto beans that have been boiled for hours on end, seasoned with bacon, beer, and spices, then mashed, fried, and called refried beans. These two sides play a crucial role in the filling nature of Tex-Mex food. It's hard to imagine the cuisine without them.

The tortilla, though, is unique in its role as both a building block of some dishes, as well as an eating utensil and food-delivery vehicle. It's an unleavened, round flatbread that is sometimes made of corn and in other instances with finely ground wheat flour. Both forms are delicious and have their roles in some incredible dishes that we'll be coverin' shortly.

THE HOLY TRINITY

TORTILLA

CORN, FLOUR, WHEAT

BEANS

PINTO, REFRIED, BLACK

RICE

SPANISH RICE

On a basic level, the tortilla is your friend at the dinner table in the way that it helps you eat with your hands—without eatin' with your hands. It's truly magical. At the beginnin' of a meal at any Tex-Mex restaurant, depending on what you order you'll be posed with the question "Corn or flour?" The server is simply askin' what flavor you'd prefer for the edible eatin' utensils that they'll be bringin' out.

For certain dishes like soup, or *caldo,* I'd recommend corn tortillas—especially if you're gonna be brave enough to give menudo a try, and I don't mean the 1980s boy band featurin' Ricky Martin. For other dishes such as carne guisada or fajitas, flour tortillas are gonna be your greatest ally.

If you're wonderin' how exactly it serves the role of utensil, well let me explain. If you're brought a bowl of

Mexican chicken soup, also known as caldo de pollo, a stack of corn tortillas allow you to sop up the delicious broth twice as fast. One hand can man the spoon and scoop up all the chunky contents of the soup, meanwhile allowing the other hand to use the corn tortilla to soak up the broth like a flat, round, edible sponge. It's efficiency at its finest.

For carne guisada, a dish consisting of stewed beef tips, the flour tortilla can be torn into little strips. These strips can then be used to pinch the food up off the plate and into your mouth. Your hand never gets dirty, which cuts down on napkin usage, which in turn is good for the environment. It's win-win, really.

I'm not forgettin' fajitas, y'all. Fajitas are made from grilled beef skirt steak. Seein' as how it's not exactly the most tender cut of beef, it's normally marinated in salty and tangy concoctions that

help tenderize things a bit. The cook'll grill 'em up and slice the steaks into little strips of meat that are then served on sizzlin'-hot metal platters along with onions, jalapeños, and green bell peppers.

Alongside the main sizzlin' platter, beans, rice, guacamole (more on that later), cheese, sour cream, and pico de gallo will also be served. It's a very DIY kinda meal, where all the parts are served separately for the consumer to piece together how they please. How exactly do you enjoy the dish, and where does the tortilla mentioned earlier come in, you ask? Hold on to your bibs because things are about to get really enjoyable.

TACOS

Tacos are one of the best things about Tex-Mex food. They can pretty much be anything you want them to be. Making them is really easy. Literally anything can be used as a fillin' in tacos, but I prefer to keep it traditional. The traditional ingredients in Tex-Mex cookin' would start with a type of meat as a base. Ground and seasoned beef, fajita strips, pork, or shredded chicken can all work. Next you'll add some toppings to round out the flavor profile. The toppings could be chopped onions, cheese, or any number of salsas. The sky is the limit.

$2.25
AL
PASTOR

CRUNCHY TACOS

On a much bigger scale, tacos can be classified in several different ways. You've got your crunchy tacos, which generally are a ground beef kinda thing, with a little shredded lettuce, cheese, and tomatoes. These get their name from the crunchy nature of their shell compared to the regular tacos we covered earlier.

STREET TACOS

The name "street tacos" doesn't exactly elicit thoughts of high-quality cuisine, but I assure you that they're exactly that. Street tacos are a special style of tacos that are generally found in trailers or taquerias that are basically taco stands on wheels. One of my favorite street tacos is a taco al pastor, which is a slow-cooked and tangy pork-filled taco with onions, cilantro, a squeeze of lime, and a couple of pineapple slices. Its flavor is as big as Texas.

At first glance, the locations that you'll get the best street tacos don't look like havens of cleanliness, but take it from me: the best tacos come from the places that don't look like the Ritz-Carlton. In fact, if you're ever at the Ritz-Carlton—or any other highfalutin place like it—and they have street tacos on the menu, just pass. Stick to the quick and cheap street tacos. There ain't no sense in fancyin' up somethin' that was never meant to be fancy.

BREAKFAST TACOS

The breakfast taco is filled with exactly what its name implies: breakfast. A multitude of things can be mixed and matched to perfection. My personal favorite is bacon and scrambled eggs with a little shredded cheese. My wife, on the other hand, is a potato, scrambled eggs, and cheese fan. Down in the Rio Grande Valley, barbacoa (shredded goat meat) is a staple for a lot of folks.

Knock yourself out mixin' and matchin' for this class of taco. There's really no wrong way to go. Around here, we like to think that breakfast tacos are the breakfast of champions. Start your day with a couple of 'em yourself, and you'll quickly fit in with the best of 'em.

FISH
$3

$2
MIGAS

GUACAMOLE

This dip is a special treat that, although delicious on its own, plays an integral role in adding value to pretty much any Tex-Mex dish (and non-Tex-Mex dish for that matter). Made by smashing ripened avocados in a bowl with diced tomatoes, lime juice, cilantro, onion, and garlic, it'll take anything you eat to the next level as a topping.

QUESO

The word for "cheese" in Spanish is queso, though to assume that this dish is solely cheese is to oversimplify it. (In some instances you'll see it referenced as chili con queso.) It's a dish consisting of melted cheese and a blend of diced peppers that together form a dip best enjoyed with an endless bowl of tortilla chips.

Ground beef and guacamole can be added, along with pico de gallo, to create what restaurants like to call queso especial (or special queso, for those of you that can't pick up on context clues).

As with the salsa we discussed in the last section, be careful around queso and chips, as they're highly addictive and will, before you know it, fill you up and ruin your appetite.

ENCHILADAS

Enchiladas are a beautiful thing. Unlike tacos, they don't need nearly the kind of construction or customization by the consumer. The work puttin' these things together takes place in the kitchen. Traditionally, this dish is made up of cheese and sometimes ground beef rolled up in a tortilla, smothered in a chili con carne sauce, and then covered in shredded cheese. All this is then baked until it's nice and melted. If you're interested in makin' some at home to try for yourself, try my Grandmother Martinez's recipe on the next page. It's the best.

Nevolena Martinez's
Famous Enchiladas

MAKES 3 to 4 servings

INGREDIENTS

2 tablespoons shortening

3 tablespoons flour

2 cups water

¼ teaspoon garlic powder

¼ teaspoon ground cumin

4 teaspoons chili powder

Salt to taste

¼ pound ground beef (optional)

Vegetable oil

8 to 10 corn tortillas

1 (8-ounce) package shredded
   Colby-Jack cheese

¼ chopped onion (optional)

DIRECTIONS

Melt shortening in a medium saucepan over medium heat. Add flour and brown the mixture for 2 to 4 minutes without burning. Add water, garlic powder, cumin, and chili powder. Use whisk to dissolve any lumps in sauce. Salt to taste. Bring to a boil, then lower heat and let simmer for 2 to 4 minutes.

Brown ground beef in a small skillet and add to sauce if desired. Remove from heat and set aside.

Preheat oven to 375°F. Pour 1 or 2 teaspoons of vegetable oil in a small skillet and place over a medium heat. Once the oil has heated, fry corn tortilla briefly in oil, turning quickly. Do not brown. Remove within 10 to 20 seconds for each. Set aside.

After heating the desired number of tortillas, assemble on a baking pan by laying tortillas flat and spreading roughly 1 tablespoon of cheese in a straight line along the middle of each. Roll tortillas up into a cylinder.

Sprinkle cheese to taste on top, and onion if you'd like, then pour enchilada sauce over the rolled tortillas. Sprinkle with more cheese. Cover baking pan with tin foil and then place in the oven. Heat for 10 minutes.

Remove from oven and serve the melted delicious mess to your friends and family along with rice and refried beans.

CHILI

There's a long-standing debate about this national dish of Texas. Folks like to argue whether beans belong in chili or not. Well let me set ya straight, right off the bat. Anyone that knows beans about chili, knows that beans don't belong in chili. There's no debatin' it really.

I apologize that I have to start off this section so sternly, but it's a cryin' shame that this dish gets ruined by the filler all the time.

Anyway, chili, or chili con carne, as it's known down south, is a delicious stew dish made up of primarily ground beef, chili peppers, and tomatoes. It was a cheap and easy meal for the workin' man, which might explain its position as the national dish of the hardest workin' land around.

Cookin' chili is a delight that every self-respectin' Texan should partake in when the weather cools and the bones get a little chilly. It warms the soul and fills the belly. The recipe I'm bestowin' upon you is from one of the granddaddies of modern-day chili, Frank X. Tolbert. In 1967, he, along with Wick Fowler, cofounded the still-runnin' International Championship Chili Cookoff that is held the first weekend of November in Terlingua, Texas. I personally know many of Frank's friends, as well as his daughter, Kathleen, and there isn't a single one of 'em that would say anyone knew more about chili than him.

Chili is serious business, and although these days its association nationally in people's minds with Texas has waned, it plays an important role in our diets. It keeps us warm when it's cold outside and fills us up when we're hungry. Perfect the art of cookin' good chili, and any old-school Texan will give you major Texas points.

The Texas
BOWL OF RED

MAKES 4 to 8 servings (depending on how hungry everyone is)

INGREDIENTS

2 to 4 ancho chilis

4 to 8 small dried red chilis (or 2 to 4 tablespoons chili powder)

3 pounds lean beef chuck, cut into bite-sized pieces

4 tablespoons vegetable oil

1 to 2 cups beef stock or water

$1/3$ cup finely chopped garlic

1 yellow onion, finely chopped

2 tablespoons ground cumin

1 tablespoon ground oregano

Salt to taste

$1/2$ cup Hungarian sweet paprika

1 or 2 fresh cilantro sprigs

DIRECTIONS

Trim the stems and remove seeds from the ancho and dried red chilis. Place the chilis and chili powder (if used) in a small saucepan and add water to barely cover. Bring to a boil, remove from the heat, cover, and let stand for 15 minutes. Transfer the chilis and their soaking water to a blender or a food processor fitted with a metal blade. Purée until smooth. Set aside.

Brown half of the beef in a large skillet in the vegetable oil over high heat for 6 to 8 minutes. Transfer the beef and juices to a heavy pot and add the puréed chilis. Place over low heat and bring to a simmer. Meanwhile, brown the remaining beef in the same manner, then transfer it and the juices to the pot. Add enough stock or water to just cover the meat. Bring to a boil, reduce the heat to low, and simmer, uncovered, for 30 minutes.

Add the garlic, onion, cumin, oregano, salt, paprika, and cilantro and continue to simmer, uncovered, stirring occasionally for another 30 minutes, until the meat is very tender. Add a little more stock or water if the mixture begins to stick or looks too dry. When the chili is ready, using a large kitchen spoon, skim any fat from the surface. Ladle into bowls and serve.

BAR-B-QUE

THE BASICS

There are a few things about bar-b-que (or BBQ) that we need to clear up right away before we proceed any further. First on that list is that all the "BBQ" you've tried outside of Texas pales in comparison to the deliciousness that you'll find here.

The second and most important for someone who ain't from Texas originally, like yourself, is to clarify what is and what ain't BBQ. There's been a tendency by some of your non-Texan friends to play fast and loose with the word "bar-b-que." Ya see, pullin' out a Weber grill and throwin' some charcoal on it don't mean you're BBQin', friend. Let's call a spade a spade. You're grillin'.

REGIONAL 'QUE

Now that we've gotten that out of the way, we can get into the nitty-gritty of fillin' your head with the basics of BBQ. As with most other things Texans identify with, there is great debate on most of the things you'll be reading next. This is purely meant to serve as a basis for your long-term education. You'll undoubtedly become an expert in your own right as time progresses and you visit BBQ joints around the state.

On a simple level, most people associate Texas BBQ with slow cooking in a smoker. What's surprising to a lot of folks that travel across the state is that each of our regions prepares BBQ slightly differently compared to the others.

RIP Pinky. You were delicious.

WEST TEXAS

West Texas is the region most often identified with the Texan mystique. There are still a great many ranches out west, and when you've got ranches, you've generally got cowboys. Bein' that the cowboys were mobile folks who didn't have the luxury of haulin' a big pit smoker everywhere, they did what they could. This often meant cookin' meat with a more direct style of heat as opposed to usin' smoke, which we'll cover shortly. Sauces are not necessarily frowned upon with this style, but they're not the focus of the meal as much as with the eastern style.

CENTRAL TEXAS

These days, the most famous style is the variety that hails from Central Texas. It's a style that relies heavily on cookin' with the smoke produced by burnin' primarily mesquite or oak wood. Sauce is not generally something you should ask for, as it's been banned in some establishments, and is looked down upon in others. Meats are meant to be flavored primarily through

IS THIS BBQ?

NO NO NO
NO NO NO

the woodsmoke and the rubs of spices and flavors before the cooking begins.

EAST TEXAS

East Texans produce a style of BBQ that tends to be, well, tender. If the meat on a rib is fallin' off the bone, the pit master has done their job correctly. Sauces are thick and generally on the sweet and tangy side of the spectrum. Bein' so close to the deep south and Louisiana, a lot of the style of cookin' found here was influenced by the descendants of slaves. As for the wood of choice for smokin', hickory reigns supreme in this region.

SOUTH TEXAS

In South Texas, also known as the Rio Grande Valley, barbacoa is a word you'll see everywhere. It's a style of BBQ that originated in Mexico and South America. Traditionally it was done by cooking the whole head of a cow in an oven made by digging a hole in the ground. The meat of the cow's head would become tender during cooking, and then scraped off and eaten.

SIDES AND BEVERAGES

I'm of the opinion that the sides you pair BBQ with can make or break the meal. Any BBQ meal without 'em is one that is incomplete.

Potato salad is an essential side that starts with a base of either mustard or mayonnaise. Since I prefer the mustard variety, that's what I'm gonna provide a recipe for in this chapter.

White bread isn't as much a side as it is a vessel for helpin' get some BBQ in your mouth. It's also great for cleanin' up your plate and soppin' up any remnants of sauces or sides that you missed with regular utensils. If the BBQ joint that you're at doesn't offer it, you're not at a BBQ joint.

BBQ beans round out the trio of basic sides that any plate should include.

They're simple, nutritious and very difficult to screw up when preparing.

Of course, I'd be amiss if I made no mention of fresh onion and pickle slices. If they're not offered where you're dinin' then stand up and calmly walk out.

The beverage I highly recommend with all BBQ, regardless of your age, is an ice-cold Big Red soda. There's somethin' perfect about it that just goes so well with all BBQ. Sweet tea is an equally good partner for all of the deliciousness we've discussed so far.

If you're of drinkin' age, an ice-cold beer is a must. Shiner Bock is my personal favorite, but Fireman's #4 from the folks at Real Ale Brewing Company in Blanco, Texas, will do ya just fine too.

	BAR-B-QUE	GRILLING
TYPE OF HEAT	Low	High
FUEL USED	Wood	Charcoal/Propane
COOKING TIME	Long time	Shorter
METHOD	Smoking	Direct heat
SKILL REQUIRED	A ton	Not much
TEXAN?	Very	Yeah

White onions

Pickles

Potato salad

Baked
beans

Sauce

White bread

Potato salad too

Macaroni and cheese

Ribs

Dr Pepper

Brisket

Ribs

Turkey

The Makin's of a Solid BBQ Spread

Sausage

THE MEATS

In Texas, we'll BBQ anything that moves and has a decent amount of meat on its bones. Although brisket is by far the meat leader, especially when you consider the kind of respect it gets, it's not the easiest meat to cook and make tender, so great brisket is a delicacy that is worth its weight in gold. Enjoyin' it chopped with sauce on a bun, sliced with onions and pickles on cheap white bread, or just straight up off the plate are all equally satisfyin'. I'll leave the decision for what suits your needs up to you. As for what other BBQ'able animals and their parts there are to enjoy, you can refer to the illustrations below. Ribs, both pork and beef, are a delicious but messy necessity, when you can get your hands on them. Chicken and turkey mostly play second fiddle compared to their bovine and pig counterparts on most plates, but some BBQ joints around our state really shine with those meats. They're not always somethin' to pass up. Sausage links are normally made with scrap meats, which are then packed into a sausage casing with a plethora of flavors. Like chicken and turkey, sausage often plays second fiddle to beef and pork BBQ, acting as more of a side. (Where else than Texas would more meat act as a side to a meat main course?)

OUR FAVORITE ANIMALS TO COOK WITH SMOKE

Goat

Turkey

Cow

Chicken

Pig

WHERE'S THE BEEF?

You may be asking yourself, "Which part of the cow is the brisket?"
Well, it's the front. See for yourself:

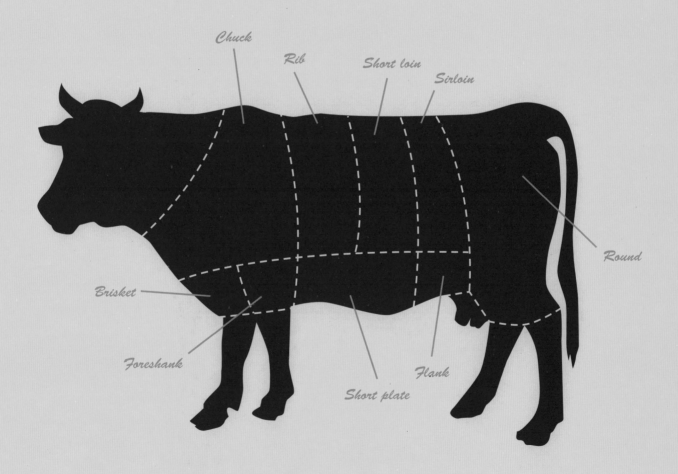

The Texas
POTATO SALAD

Makes 6 to 8 servings

Ingredients

1½ pounds russet potatoes
4 eggs
¾ cup celery, diced
½ cup onion, minced
½ cup dill salad cubes
2 tablespoons dill pickle juice
2½ tablespoons yellow mustard
½ cup mayonnaise
Salt and ground pepper to taste

DIRECTIONS

Boil potatoes in salted water until they are practically fallin' apart. Drain in a colander and then return to warm pot to dry out a bit.

Hard-boil eggs, peel, and smash into pieces, including yolk. Mix with celery, onion, dill salad cubes, and pickle juice, then add in mustard and mayonnaise until consistency is not quite firm, but not quite runny. Add salt and pepper to taste.

WILD GAME

With a state as big as ours, there's a plethora of animals roamin' the countryside (or your backyard) and our waters that are ripe for the grillin', fryin', or smokin'. Following is a visual guide to the various animals that are perfect for this.

WILD BOAR

These invasive animals aren't exactly the prettiest, or easiest to track down by foot, but bein' the inventive types that we are, we're usin' helicopters these days to attack from above, just like Mother Nature intended. If you shoot one, they're smelly and not super-easy to clean, but their back strap is pretty good pork.

GOOD *for* SHOOTIN' *and* COOKIN'!

WHITETAIL DEER

The whitetail deer is fantastic eatin', but the hardest part of gettin' one is the gettin' one part. Through the not-so-natural selection of our huntin' them, the only ones that are still alive are the super-skittish types that were smart enough to run the first time they heard a Texan whisper, "Hey, Bill! I think I see one. Hand me my rifle."

That bein' said, if you do happen to shoot one (you'll need a huntin' license), their meat is delicious and great for makin' sausage out of.

QUAIL Small birds that are easy to take down with a shotgun and patience. They're especially good when paired with a beer and bacon to wrap them in while grillin'.

WITH ALL THESE TASTY CRITTERS JUST LYIN' AROUND HOW IS A GIRL SUPPOSED TO CHOOSE JUST ONE?!

FISH

Pretty much all the fish in Texas are edible, though I can't personally say I've ever eaten alligator gar. My favorite part about goin' fish huntin' (also known as fishin') is all the sittin' and drinkin' you get to do. Once you do catch somethin', fryin' it or simply searin' it with butter and garlic is the way to go.

ALLIGATOR

You'll find these unfriendly fellas primarily in the bayous and waters of East Texas, but they make for good eatin'. I don't recommend tryin' to wrassle one yourself, though. Find the nearest Cajun and ask them for assistance.

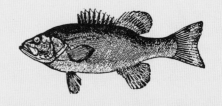

DUCK

You can't go wrong with eatin' duck. Good huntin' of these waterfowl can be found throughout the state wherever tall grass and water meet. If you think you'll be leanin' towards redneck inclinations while you develop as a Texan, please note that shootin' the ducks that are found at city parks is frowned upon.

RABBIT Rabbit are plentiful in Texas, especially in the Southwest region, where they're known for tearin' up crops and eatin' all the deer corn. Good for tasty, albeit small, meals.

Dove See "Quail"

The Texas
PECAN PIE

I can't go through this whole chapter and not make a single mention of dessert. The king of desserts in Texas is pecan pie. It was deemed the official pie by our legislature, which is about as official as you can get. Personally, I don't think a slice of pie should be enjoyed without a scoop of Blue Bell Ice Cream Homemade Vanilla, but that's just me.

MAKES 2 pies

INGREDIENTS
1 stick of butter
4 eggs
1 cup chopped pecans
1 cup corn syrup
1 cup semisweet chocolate chips
¾ cup sugar
¼ cup brown sugar
1 teaspoon vanilla extract
Pinch of all-purpose flour
2 regular pie shells
Whole pecans

DIRECTIONS

Melt butter and combine with eggs in mixing bowl.

Combine all other ingredients, except pie shells.

Divide mixture evenly between the 2 pie shells. Make sure to scoop from the bottom of the mixing bowl to evenly spread the chocolate chips. Sprinkle a few whole pecans on top; for best results, arrange pecans in the shape of a lone star.

Cook in oven at 350°F for 35 to 40 minutes.

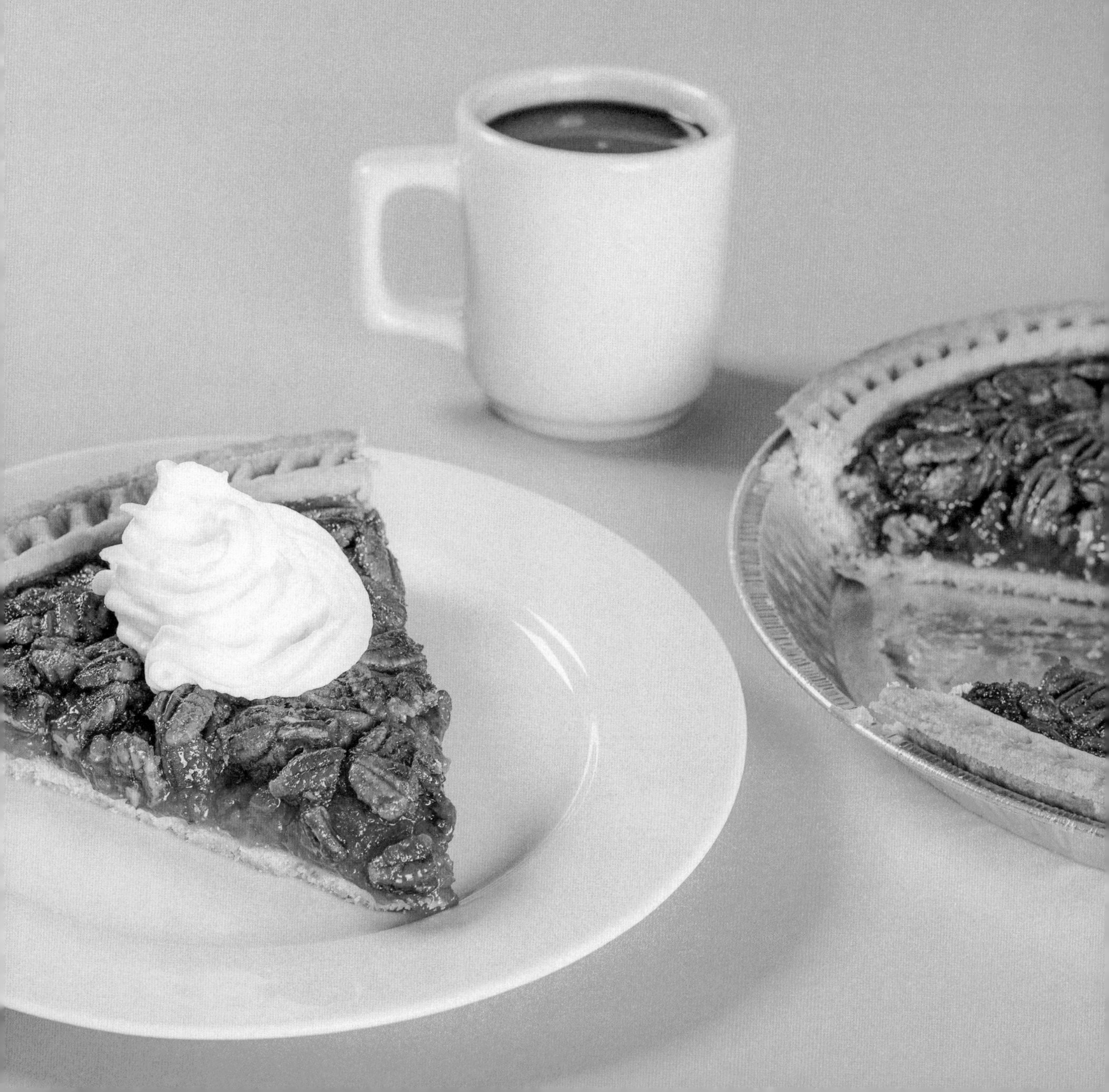

Texas Two-Step

Since Texas is a meltin' pot of cultures, it only makes sense that one of the best drinks around is actually two drinks from two cultures. I like to call this the Texas Two-Step, as you can see in the giant text above. It consists of a good shot of tequila followed by an ice-cold Texas beer. If you're short on cash, the good shot of tequila can be substituted with a cheap shot of tequila. Just beware of headaches ahead.

Mouth

Neck

Cold beer

Shot glass

Tequila

BEVERAGES

BEER

These days, there are a lot of great brewers poppin' up all over the state that draw on the strong German, Czech, and other cultural influences in Texas. There are far too many to list here, but suffice it to say that you should try them all. Don't waste your time on those imports from St. Louis or the Rockies. There are plenty of Texas brewers who'd be happy to have your business. It's important to support these folks, because in the event that we did ever secede from the rest of the United States, you wouldn't want to be without a supply of beer, now would ya?

WINE

It should be noted that Central Texas is home to many wineries that are on par (and in my opinion better) than those you'll find in Tuscany or the Sonoma Valley. As it turns out, Central Texas's climate and landscape is perfect for growin' grapes. The Texas wine industry is growin' in size and stature every year. Along US Highway 290 between Johnson City and Fredericksburg you'll find countless wineries that are ready and waitin' for your arrival.

ICED TEA

Home-brewed tea is a special thing that you just can't imitate. Most Texans prefer it sweet, which is how I prefer it as well. Go big on the sugar and you'll never look back.

HOW TO ENJOY: It's a satisfyin' beverage pretty much all the time. Hot summer days on the porch are a highly recommended time to imbibe.

PAIRINGS: All foods.

Dr Pepper

Those folks over in Atlanta like to make a big dang deal about how pervasive and old Coca-Cola is, but at the end of the day, Dr Pepper was first, and it was invented in Waco, Texas, which makes it better by default. It's the oldest soda in the United States, and in my humble opinion, the best.

HOW TO ENJOY: Pretty much anywhere, anytime.

PAIRINGS: All foods.

PRO TIP: Swap out Coca-Cola for Dr Pepper in your coke floats. You can thank me later.

SANGRIA WINE

Sangria is one of the best adult beverages to enjoy in Texas on a hot summer day. There are a million different ways to make it too, which allows for a lot of experimentin' in your kitchen laboratory. Simply speakin', it's primarily a wine with chopped fruits, simple syrup, and brandy mixed together in a large pitcher.

How to enjoy: It's a great party drink when you've got a handful of friends comin' over.

Texas musician Jerry Jeff Walker says it best in his song "Sangria Wine":

My friends come over Saturday night
Man it's nice to make up some sangria wine
It's organic and it comes from the vine
It's also legal and it gets you so high
And I love that sangria wine
Love to drink it with old friends of mine
Yeah I love to get drunk with friends of mine
When we're drinkin' that ole' sangria wine

Pairings: It's enjoyable with meals, but it's more of a social drink in my opinion. As mentioned, there are a lot of ways to make it your own, but one of my favorite recipes follows.

Saturday Night
SANGRIA WINE

MAKES 1 pitcher

INGREDIENTS

1½ cup blackberries

½ cup simple syrup

1 (750 milliliter) bottle red wine (might
I suggest a Texas Shiraz?)

¼ cup cognac or regular brandy

3 peaches, pitted and sliced (might I recommend Fredericksburg peaches?)

DIRECTIONS

Cook berries and simple syrup in a medium
saucepan over medium heat, stirring constantly for 5 minutes. When berries lighten and syrup thickens, pull from heat and set aside.

Pour wine into a pitcher or other large serving con-
tainer. Add cognac, peaches, and the syrup and
berry mixture. Cover with pitcher top and refriger-
ate for at least 5 to 6 hours so flavors can "edu-
cate" one another. Drink, dance, and be Texan.

Mexican martini   *Margarita*

The margarita is an adult drink we have our neighbors to the south to thank for. The standard recipe consists of tequila, triple sec, and lime juice. It's served on the rocks or blended into a frozen slush-type drink. Depending on your taste, you might enjoy a bit of salt added to the rim of your glass for a bit extra tang. Speakin' of glass, they're tasty in any-shaped cup, but margaritas are generally served in glassware like that pictured on the facing page.

If the margarita strikes your fancy, then you might be a fan of its bigger, stronger, older sibling, the Mexican martini. As its name implies it's served in a martini glass, but garnished with an olive or two and salt on the rim. In reality, it's basically a margarita with a larger serving size and a couple more ingredients.

CLASSIC MARGARITA

MAKES 1 serving

INGREDIENTS
2 ounces tequila
1 ounce triple sec
Juice of 2 limes
Salt and lime slice for garnish

DIRECTIONS
Mix all ingredients along with ice in a shaker. Serve in a chilled glass with a salted rim and lime slice garnish.

How to enjoy: Yet another great summer drink. I think it pairs well with Tex-Mex music and sandy beaches, but frankly they're good anywhere, anytime.

Pairings: Tex-Mex cuisine is the best pairing for this beverage.

Note: As with any cocktail, there are a million ways to flavor this drink to your likin'. Around the state you'll find jalapeño-, strawberry-, or sangria-infused margaritas. Your assignment is to spend some time researchin' these yourself.

MEXICAN MARTINI

MAKES 1 serving

INGREDIENTS
2 ounces añejo tequila
1 ounce Cointreau
1 ounce Sprite
1 ounce orange juice
1½ ounces lime juice
½ ounce green olive brine from jar
Salt to taste
Green olives for garnish

DIRECTIONS
Mix all ingredients, except salt and green olives, in a drink shaker along with ice cubes. Shake thoroughly. Salt rim of martini glass and garnish glass with olives. Serve in shaker, allowing guests to serve themselves via shaker and strainer.

How to enjoy: Though they can be found statewide these days, they're primarily found in Austin, so enjoy while keepin' it weird.

Pairings: Tex-Mex foods are perfecto.

DRIVIN' TEXAN

Sample Material:

TEXAS ROAD TRIP SIMULATOR • DIRECTIONS • THE WAVE

THE DESOLATE HIGHWAY WAVE • SUMMER DRIVIN' • WINTER DRIVIN'

Drivin' in Texas isn't especially hard if you're prepared. We've got a lot of roads here. 675,580 to be exact. In fact, if you were to drive all of them from start to finish, it would be the equivalent of traveling to the moon and back and then almost back to it once more.

The point of tellin' ya all this is to explain that I wouldn't get too hung up about the physical distance between two locations. Our state is so dang big that the only measurement that matters is time. The shortest distance between two points can be found by just drivin' as fast as humanly possible.

Texas Road Trip Simulator

To give you an idea of what it's like to drive in Texas, we've built this highly scientific Texas Road Trip Simulator right smack dab in to the middle of this book. It'll give you an idea of how it feels to drive between San Antonio and El Paso, which is one of my favorite drives in Texas.

To get the full effect, we recommend using the simulator while drinkin' a large Dr Pepper, turning a small box fan in your direction, and puttin' a little bit of George Strait on the radio.

To use the simulator, simply turn the next series of pages slowly while wondering "Are we there yet?" over and over in your head.

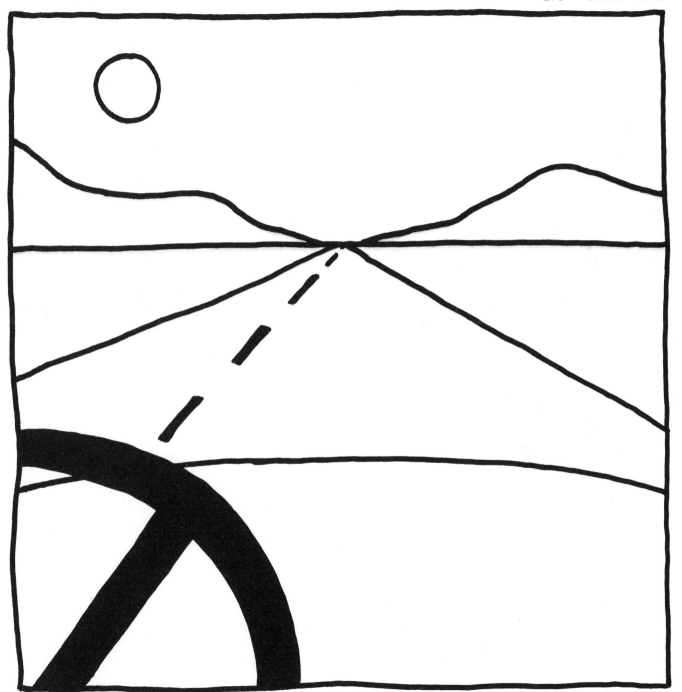

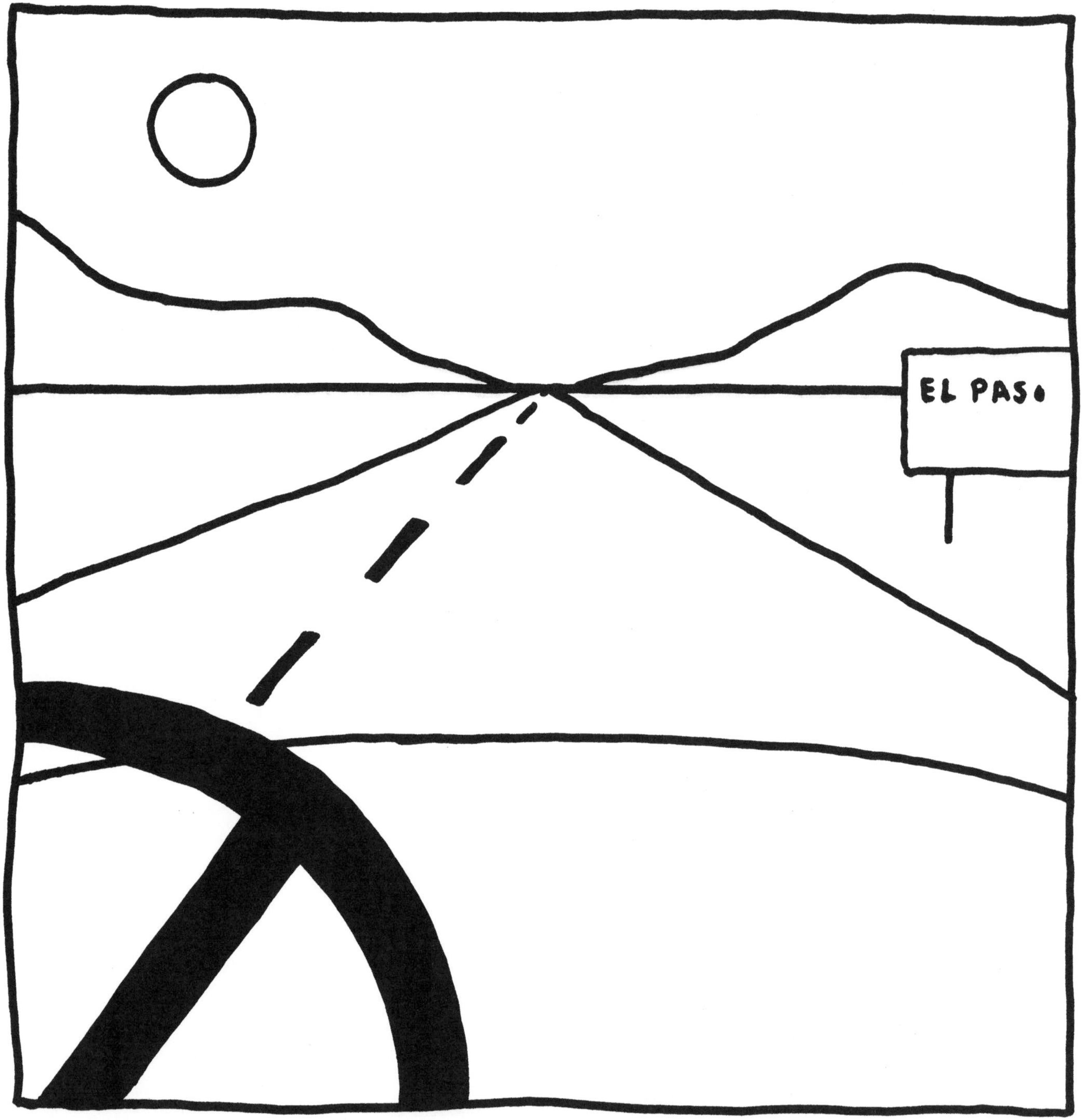
EL PASO

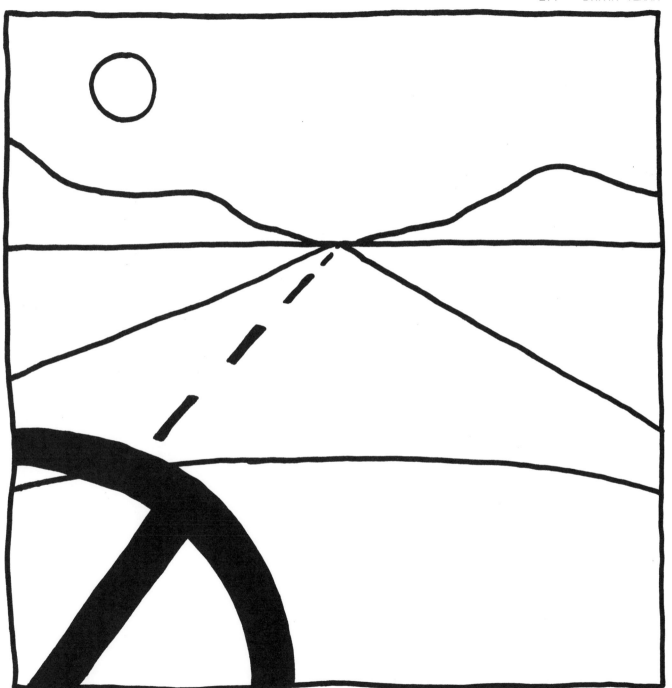

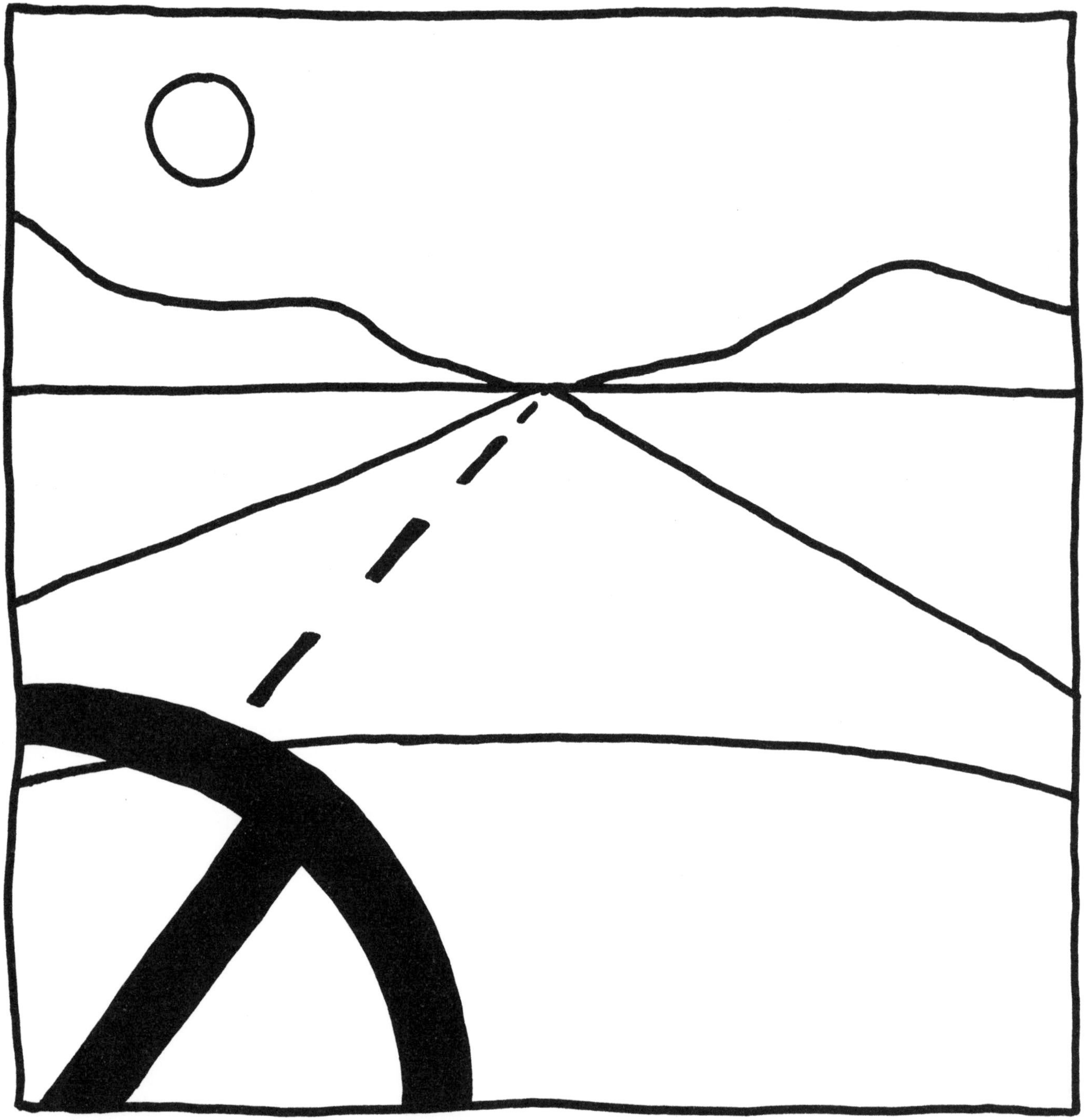

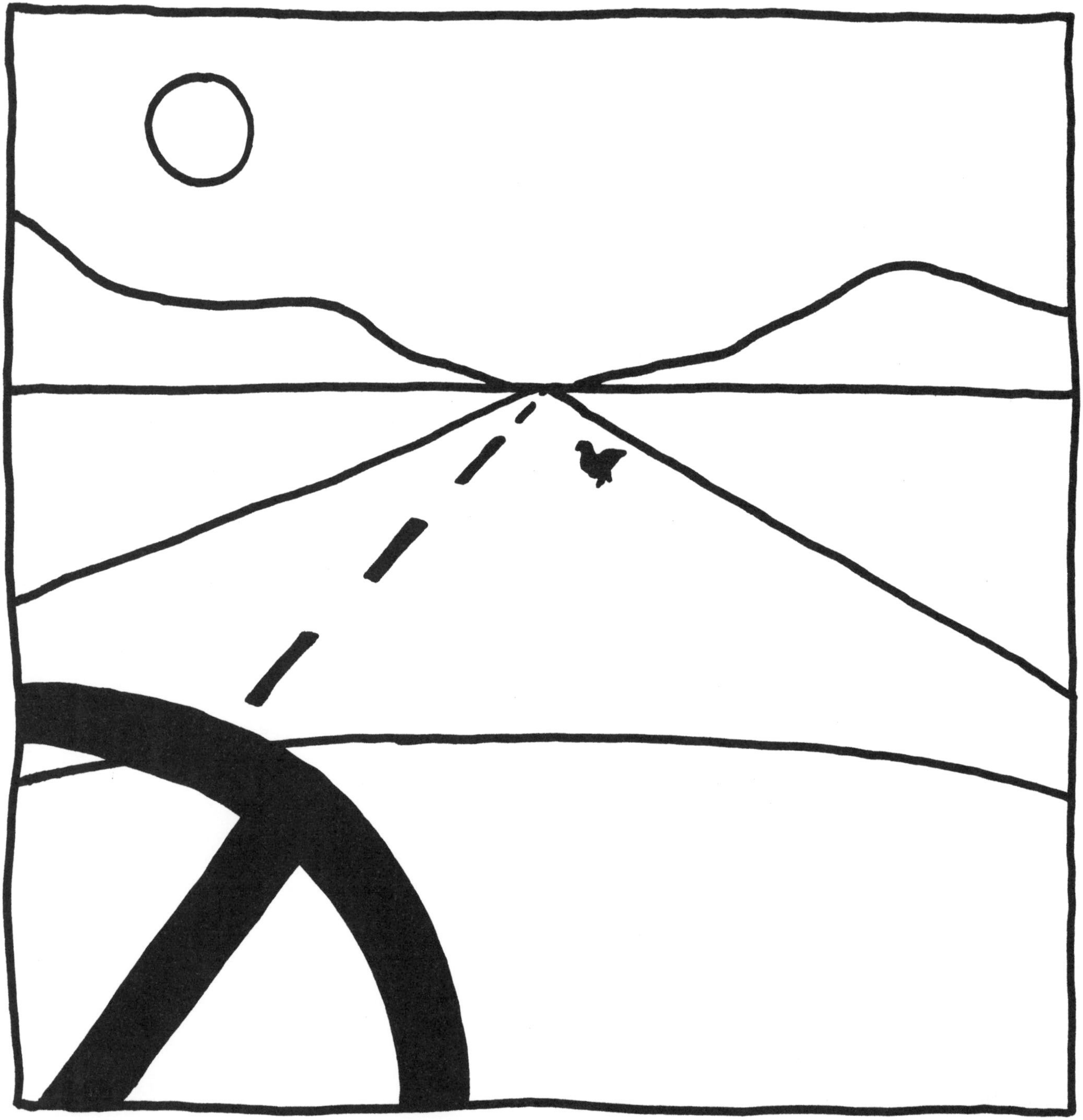

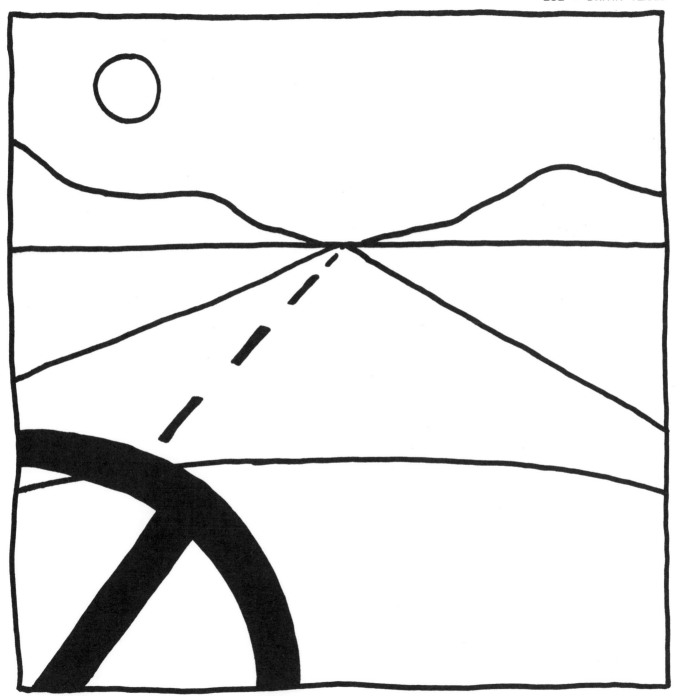

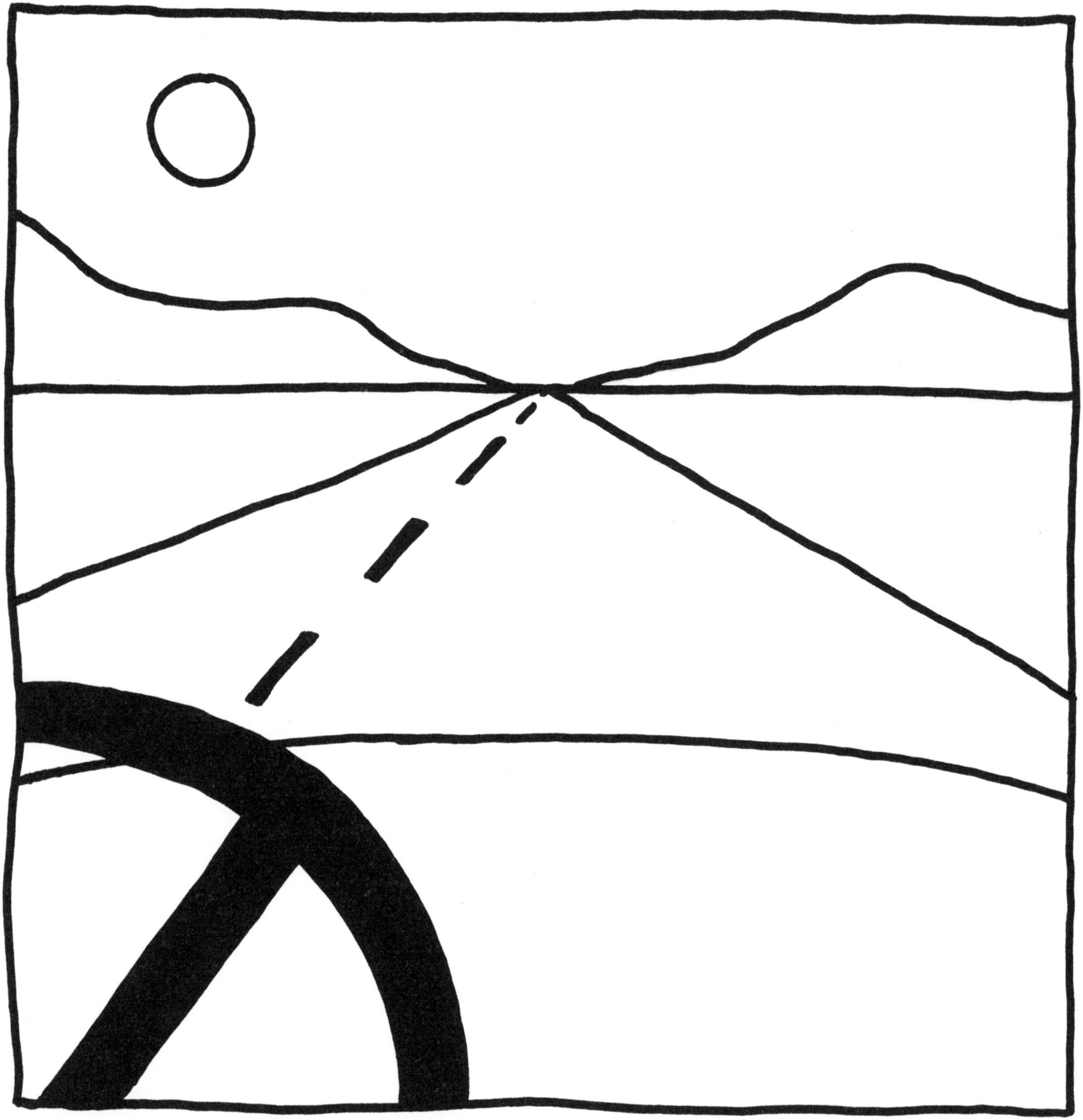

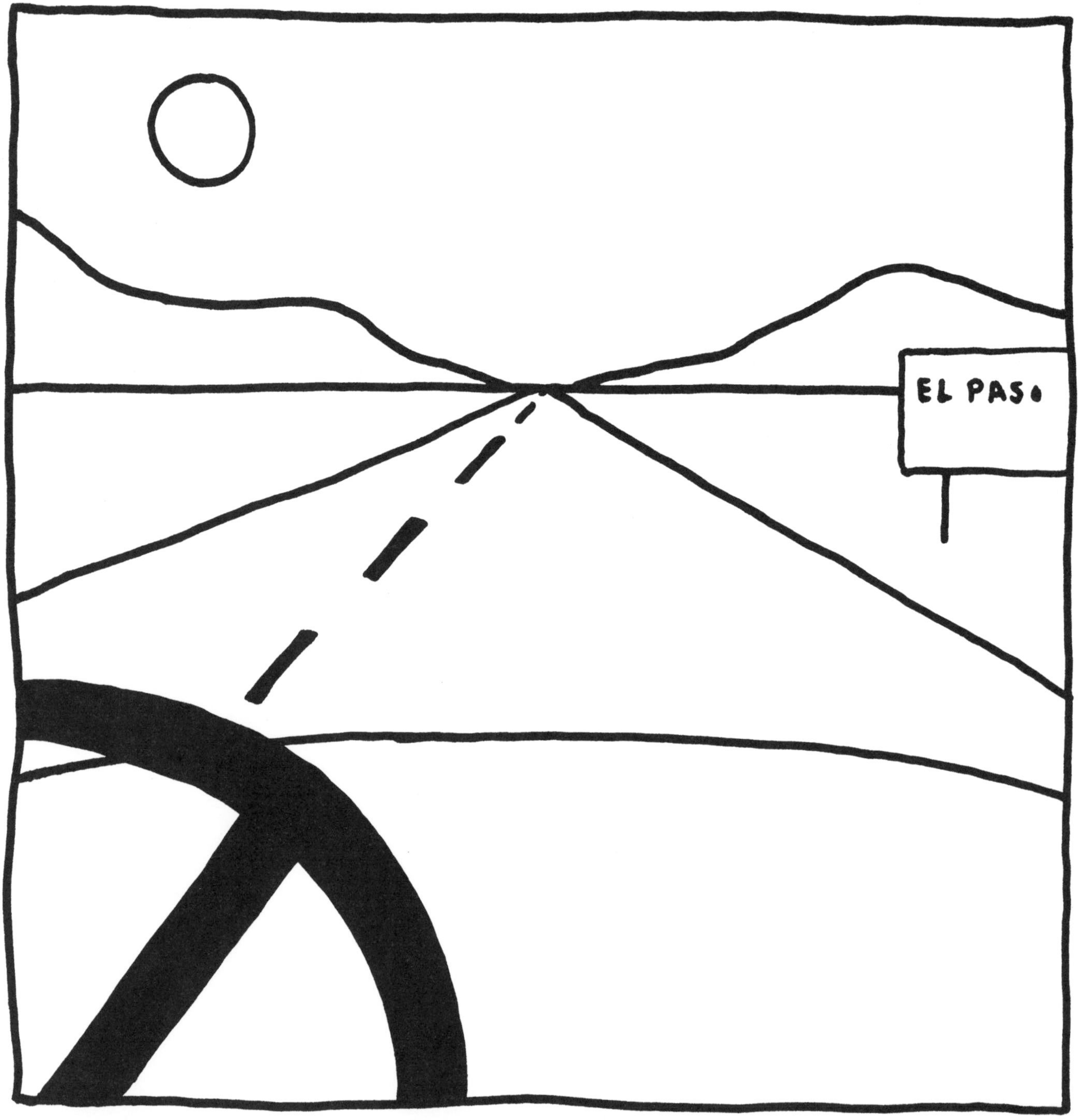
EL PASO

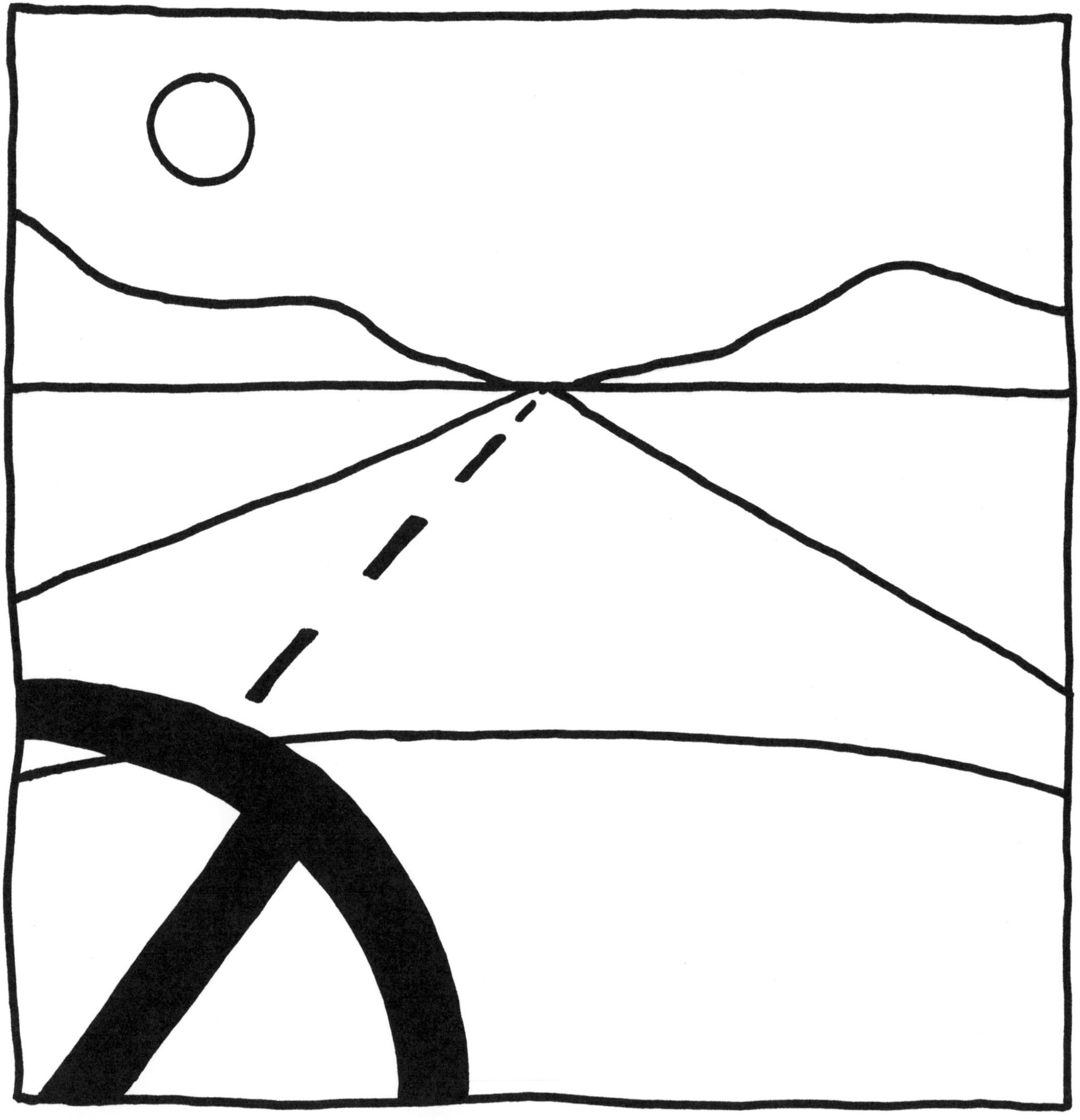

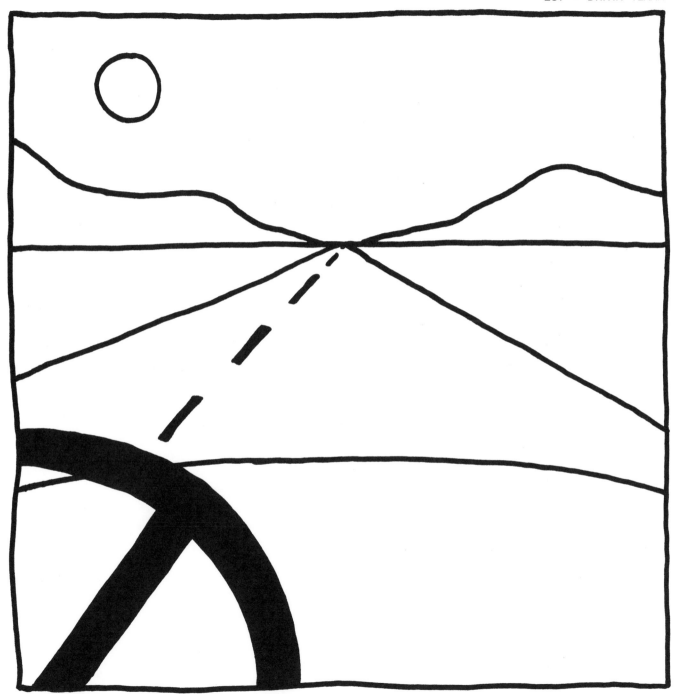

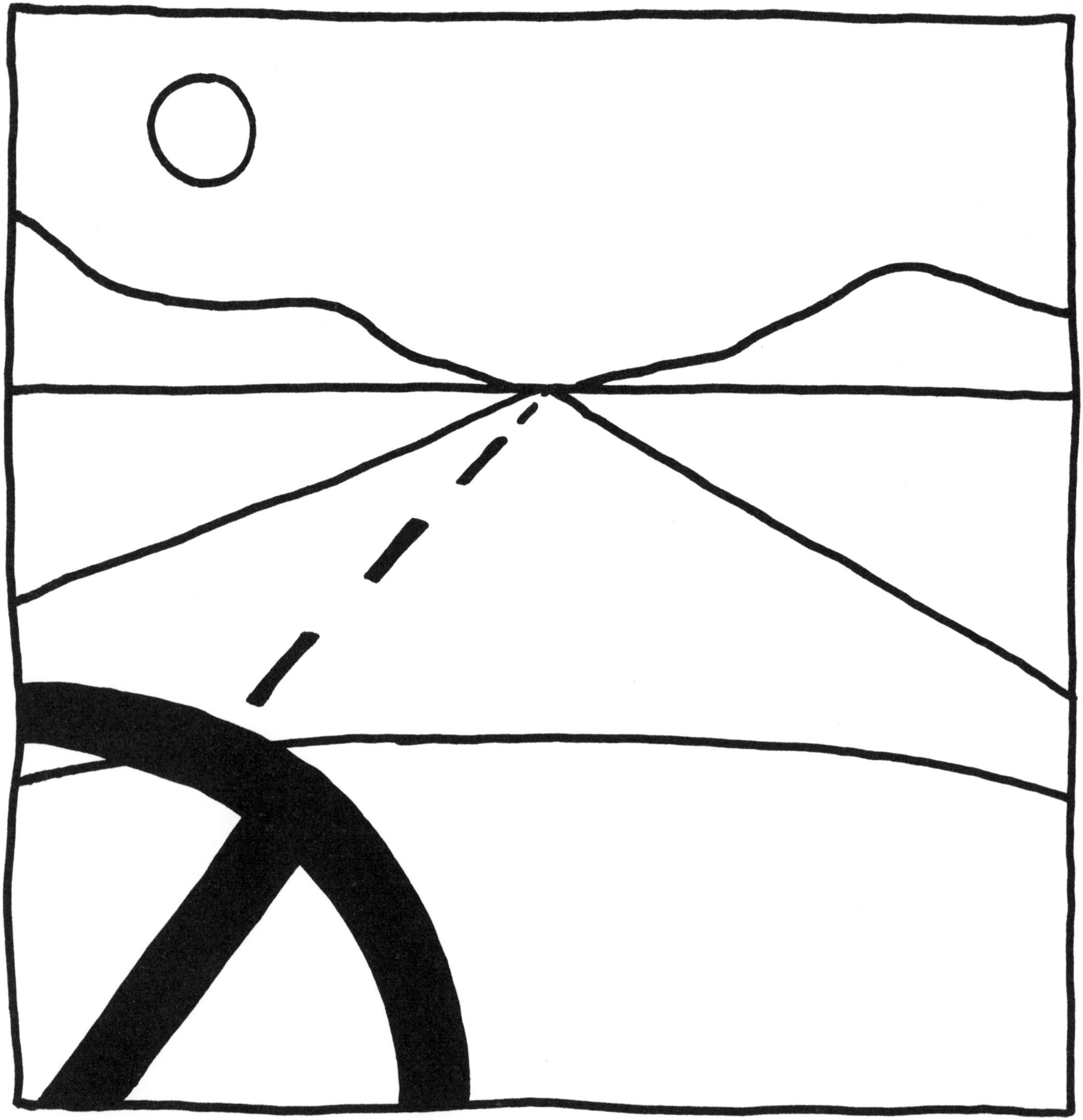

Congratulations. You've successfully experienced our Texas Road Trip Simulator. It has accurately* portrayed 1/829th of the trip. To get the full experience, repeat the previous process an additional 828 times.

* Not at all accurate.

The Vanity Plate

Few things are as Texan as really obnoxious license plates. There are a plethora of ways to show your state pride, but if you want to keep it simple, turn the Texas up on those plates.

Most likely belongs to an obnoxiously large truck

DIREC
TIONS

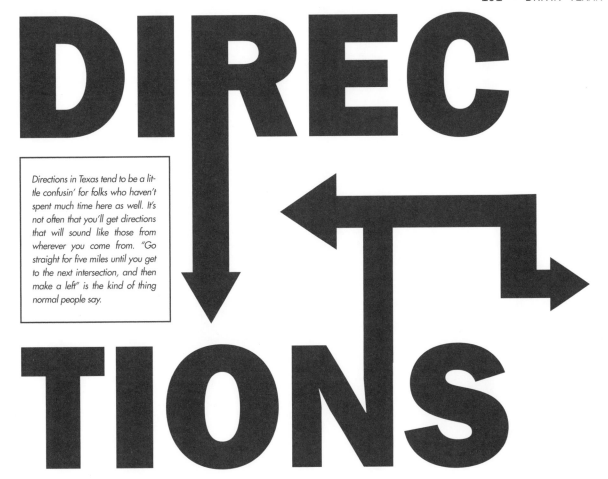

Directions in Texas tend to be a little confusin' for folks who haven't spent much time here as well. It's not often that you'll get directions that will sound like those from wherever you come from. "Go straight for five miles until you get to the next intersection, and then make a left" is the kind of thing normal people say.

TEXANS ARE GOING TO GIVE YOU DIRECTIONS THAT SOUND LIKE THIS:

"Come on down by headin' from your place 'til you see that place with all the trucks on the corner. Turn towards the water tower and drive past the big ol' farm with funny little goats on it. Once you pass my uncle's place on the side, follow the wiggly road another click or two 'til you see that joint with the awesome tamales. When you smell the tamales, you're almost there. Our place is the third one with the boot on the fence post. If you get to the feed store, you've gone too far."

For starters, phrases like "come on down," "come on up," and "come on over" all mean "come here" but aren't necessarily meant to imply the direction of travel regardless of where you're startin' and where you're finishin'. You could be at the South Pole and drivin' straight north to Dallas and some Texan will still tell you to "come on down."

AVOID ROAD RAGE
WITH *the* "WAVE"

It's easy to prevent road rage in Texas. For the most part, Texans continue our tradition of friendliness behind the wheel. The only instance in which you'll find yourself on the unfriendly side of a single finger salute will be if you do somethin' just plain unfriendly.

The best example I could give would be if you were tryin' to merge in to a lane full of vehicles. You're waitin' patiently and then a friendly Texan lets ya in. If you are allowed in to the lane and you don't acknowledge your appreciation for this gesture, you'll absolutely find yourself to be on the receiving end of some Texan nonhospitality.

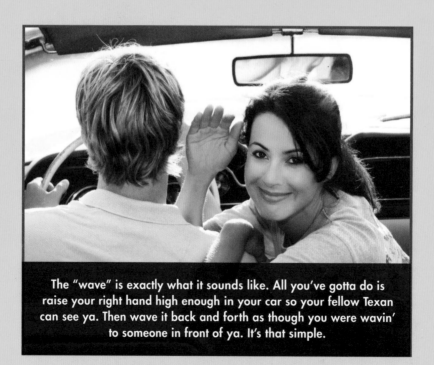

The "wave" is exactly what it sounds like. All you've gotta do is raise your right hand high enough in your car so your fellow Texan can see ya. Then wave it back and forth as though you were wavin' to someone in front of ya. It's that simple.

1. Listening to Waylon.

2. Friendly wave to oncoming car.

3. Back to Waylon.

The Desolate Highway Wave

Along the same lines as bein' friendly when someone does somethin' nice for ya in traffic, us Texans like to show our friendliness at 70 mph too. If you happen to find yourself cruisin' down the wide open road and pass another Texan, don't be alarmed if you see them raise a single finger up from their steering wheel just as you pass. Dependent upon which finger they're usin', they're probably just tellin' ya "howdy". Here's how this little wave works.

SUMMER DRIVIN'

The process of drivin' in the summer really isn't all that different from drivin' any other time of the year. You've still gotta keep it between the lines and avoid hittin' anything. The main difference is the heat. For the most part, when folks think about the dangers of drivin', they think about other people and hazards on the road. During the summertime, your main concern should be about your own dang car.

For starters, a car left in the Texas sun for more than a few minutes turns into a portable baking oven. The air inside of it instantly approaches face melting temperatures. The steering wheel will be hot enough to melt and fuse iron. Lastly and most importantly, the seats and metal seat belt buckles heat to the same temperature as the surface of the sun.

How can you safeguard yourself against these piping hot materials lurking inside every Texas vehicle? First off, you'll

"I'm ready to drive!"
—Michelle, Austin

absolutely want to avoid purchasing a dark vehicle. Black cars are only for sick folks who like pain. Secondly, shaded parking spots are your friend. Thirdly, cracking your windows and throwin' up a snazzy windshield shade can do wonders for keepin' the heat in check. Fourthly, you should avoid cars with leather seats at all costs. If you're unable to avoid said vehicles with leather seats, then make sure you're either wearin' jeans or your health insurance has great coverage for third degree burns.

"My ride's here!"

The last line of defense, would be to carry around a pair of oven mitts with you. This way you can open your door handle and put on your seat belt without destroying your precious hands. They'll also come in super handy for movin' the baking sheet of cookies you could have baked on your dashboard while your car sat in the sun.

RAIN DRIVIN'

Drivin' while it's rainin' is very similar to winter drivin'. The roads end up slicker than snot on a doorknob. Add to that the fact that Texans aren't used to seein' rain and you're in for a mess. It's not unreasonable to see people pullin' over and takin' pictures of the liquid fallin' from the sky. Keep your eyes on the road, turn your windshield wipers up, and just keep on drivin' like you would wherever it is that you're from.

WINTER DRIVIN'

As we've covered in previous chapters, it doesn't get too cold here in Texas, so when it comes to drivin' in things like sleet and snow, we have little to no experience. All you need to know is that it's in your best interest to just hunker down and stay home the next time you see that kinda weather in the forecast. If you must go out on the road, be ready for drivers on the road who have about the same dexterity and coordination as a buffalo on roller skates.

Ultimately, if you take anything away from this book, we ask that you always go big or go home. Whether it's waving an obnoxiously large Texas flag in front of landmarks that aren't in Texas, or putting the largest wheels you are legally allowed to put on a truck, you must go big.

The Texas mystique wasn't built on mediocrity and small stuff. It wasn't even built on above-average or medium-sized stuff. It was built on the overwhelming and relentless nature of our pride and attitude. Overbearing pride that annoys those who don't understand it is our modus operandi.

God Bless Texas

ACKNOWLEDGMENTS

Dear reader, if you're reading this, you've gotten out. And if you've come this far maybe you're willing to come a little further.

I'd like to thank my editor, Bob Cooper, for obliging every one of my and Cody's requests for "one more day" when we reached all of our design deadlines. I promise we were working on the book and not out boozing. I got all of the drinkin' out of the way when I wrote this thing.

I've gotta throw a big thanks to my folks, Juan and Les Sauceda, for always bein' supportive of me throughout the years, including that one time my dad's face ended up on *The Colbert Report.* I promise I had no idea you were going to be the butt of a joke on national TV.

Thanks to my little brother Chris for being a great dad to my niece and giving me a good example for when my daughter would eventually be born.

Thanks to George Jones for your infinite wisdom. Even in death you continue to keep me grounded.

Thanks to the Butler Bros for giving me my start in the creative world even though I had zero experience and was studying political science. Workin' for y'all was pretty all right.

Gracias to my employees at Sauceda Industries for keepin' the lights on while I was away all those times workin' on this book. I promise the book is real. It wasn't just an excuse to get out of that hot warehouse and spend time in the A/C at my office.

Thanks to John Ruszkiewicz for the years of friendship and great conversations about NASA. Also, thanks for letting me house-sit that one summer. Sorry again about Carl's shedding. Most importantly, since this was my first book, thanks for the advice on how to write the manuscript and for helping to make sure my publisher was legit and not some random Nigerian bank transfer scam.

Thanks to all of the followers of Texas Humor. All the support you've shown our company over the years has been incredible. You've allowed me to have one of the coolest jobs out there.

Thanks to Sam and Clare Zaborowski for all the support over the years and the endless number of conversations where you talk me off of whatever cliff I'm currently standing next to. Also, thanks for all the pies.

Thanks to Grandma Rita for tellin' me to find my bliss. Turns out I was livin' in the middle of it all this time.

Thanks to that lady that let me into her lane on I-35 today. I really didn't think I'd be able to get over in time to make my exit. You were a real lifesaver.

Thanks to Randy Taylor for the endless jokes.

Thanks for nothin', Stu Taylor. You're cool though, Meg. Love ya.

Thanks to Brad and Tina for letting me store the Horseshoe Lounge shuffleboard while you prepare for the new bar. I don't know what I would have done with no shuffleboard time these last few months.

Thanks to Adam Voorhes for telling me that I should become a photographer. Thanks to Robin Finlay for giving me my first real job as one.

Thanks to the Nall brothers for inducting me in the Clear Berets. It's been a great family to be a part of.

Thanks to Jim Tugmon for all the twisted margaritas over the years. You sure make a stiff drink.

Thanks to Jack Potter for stayin' up late drinkin' whiskey with me.

Thanks to Hayden for taking what may arguably be the least appetizing set of photos for the food section of this book. You really nailed it.

Thanks to Cody "Larry" Haltom for all the hard work puttin' this bad boy together. The check is in the mail.

Thanks to Richard Lopez at RiverCity Sportswear for badgering me until I started buying products from y'all. It's made a world of a difference in our lives.

To Priss, Carl, and Winslow, I'm finished with this sucker. Thank y'all for being so understanding during my crazy work-related pursuits. I'm comin' home.

To Evie, everything I do is because of you. Love you, baby girl.

DISCLAIMERS

I take no responsibility for any personal injuries that may occur due to advice taken from this book. I also make no claims to the accuracy of anything written in the preceding pages. That being said, all sales are final.

Before you write me to complain; yes I know that this book is missing anything about tamales; modern Texas history; guns; the Battleship *Texas*; 85 m.p.h. speed limits; Whataburger; Amarillo; Alpine; Rip Torn; whiskey; Selena; Tejano music; the Texas Tornados; Little Joe; Willie Nelson; Barton Springs; the Frio River; South Padre Island; deer huntin'; Gilley's; Bud; Sissy; Billy Bob's; mechanical bulls; Lil' Troy; Swishahouse; the Astros; Hakeem the Dream; Marvin Zindler; the Best Little Whorehouse in Texas; ZZ Top; the Gristmill; floatin' the river; AstroWorld; Fiesta Texas; Fiesta San Antonio; the palm trees in the RGV; Freddy Fender; Czech Stop; the Zavala flag; José Navarro; Ricky Williams; Mack Brown; the Horseshoe Lounge; La Virgen de San Juan; Kris; Waylon; Jack Ingram; the La Porte Bulldogs; that giant football stadium in Allen; Ann Richards; W; the Kemah Boardwalk; the Astrodome; JerryWorld; Emmitt Smith; the Spurs; Mark Cuban; the Pine Curtain; the Tyler Rose; the Rangerettes; Bevo; Leslie; that guy who rides a bike while only wearing a G-string in Austin; raspas; that goat in Lajitas that

used to drink a ton of beer; Terlingua; Hondo Crouch; Luckenbach; Hunt; Carrizo Springs; the oil fields of Eagle Ford; Presidio County; Littlefield; Dalhart; the Panhandle; the Guadalupe Mountains; Sam Houston Race Park; Texas Motor Speedway; Waxahachie; Buc-ee's; Schlitterbahn; kolaches; La Porte; the 12th Man; Johnny Football; I-45; the Alamodome; Coach Pop; the Gage Hotel; El Niño; Lake Travis; Sweet Leaf Tea; Shiner Bock; Real Ale; Fireman's #4; fajitas; queso recipes; salsa recipes; taco recipes; *King of the Hill;* I-10; Big Bend National Park; Big Bend Ranch State Park; Balmorhea State Park; Marfa; Fort Davis; Fort Stockton; Wick Fowler; Frank X. Tolbert; Ima Hogg; Jim Hogg; Rick Perry; Anything for Selenas; Corpus; H-E-B; Delia's Tamales; border checkpoints; Texan passports; 6th Street; the Fort Worth Stockyards; Dallas bein' all Dallas; Tim Duncan bein' old as all get-out; the Alpine Cowboy Poetry Gathering; George Strait's retirement; Walter Cronkite; the mockingbird; other things you can make with pecans; the Guadalupe River; San Marcos Airport; the peacocks living in south Austin; Brian Hyde; Ben Heasty; Sonja Angelo; Georgia Zaborowski; Samuel Zaborowski; Max Zaborowski; why riding a motorcycle in Texas is a horrible idea; the best way to avoid fire ants; how much fire ants suck; Pantera; calf scrambles; Rodeo

Austin; how humid it is in Houston; Buffalo Bayou; the Austin bats; how no one likes hockey; playin' horseshoes; playin' washers; Globe Life Park in Arlington; Nolan Ryan; Jeff Bagwell; the Killer B's; Clyde "The Glide" Drexler; why "affluenza" is the dumbest thing ever; the World's Largest Pecan; the Lost Pines fire; Texas edition trucks; the Josh Abbott Band; how if you're gonna play in Texas you've gotta have a fiddle in the band; Spencer Highway; Gringo's; Jimmy Changa's; Johnny Tamale's; Coach Taylor; *Friday Night Lights;* Clear eyes, full hearts, can't lose; crawfish boils; the Houston Ship Channel; that *Bernie* movie; *Dazed and Confused*; Asleep at the Wheel; Pat Green; Roger Creager; *Texas Monthly*; Brian Phillips; how Geoff Peveto couldn't design his way out of a paper bag; Momma; trains; trucks; prison; or gettin' drunk.

Believe me, it saddened me to not be able to include any of that either. That's why you should be on the lookout for *Y'all Need This Book, Part Dos: The Republic Strikes Back*, due in stores some time before 2020.

All complaints and comments should be sent to:

Professional Texan
PO Box 40879
Austin, TX 78704

CREDITS

All photos are by Jay B Sauceda and all illustrations are by Cody Haltom, or in the public domain, except as listed below by page number.

8: RandyStephensPhotography/istockphoto.com
12: nkbimages/istockphoto.com
20, 32, 77 (frog), 138 (pecan), 161 (cowgirl): Austin Jennings
22: David Sucsy/istockphoto.com (Capitol), Vepar5/istockphoto.com (ballot box), State of Texas Archives (state seal)
23: Yuri_Arcurs/istockphoto.com (man), DigtialStorm/istockphoto.com (pie chart)
24: eyegelb/istockphoto.com (petri dish), twilightproductions/istockphoto.com (oil pump), Ysbrand Cosijn/istockphoto.com (man), kuriputosu/istockphoto.com (calculator), Kagenmi/istockphoto.com (eagle), 1MoreCreative/istockphoto.com (math)
25: NASA/Jay B Sauceda
26–29, 98 (hat), 102, 147, 148, 150, 154, 158, 163, 164, 168, 190: Hayden Spears
33: wolv/istockphoto.com
34: ivanastar/istockphoto.com (teddy bear)
36: Jay B Sauceda (Declaration of Independence)
42, 66, 134, 172: Dean_Fikar/istockphoto.com
44: ilbusca/istockphoto.com
46: msderrick/istockphoto.com (Stu Taylor), Marilyn Nieves/istockphoto.com (Chato)
47: Kemter/istockphoto.com (man), BahadirTanriover/istockphoto.com (cow)
48: YinYang/istockphoto.com
50: GetUp_Studio/istockphoto.com (1st row, left & middle), xelf/istockphoto.com (1st row, right), WendellandCarolyn/istockphoto.com (2nd row, left), Susan Chiang/istockphoto.com (2nd row, middle), Johnny Greig/istockphoto.com (2nd row, right), Juanmonino/istockphoto.com (3rd row, left), IndyEdge/istockphoto.com (3rd row, middle), Susan H. Smith/istockphoto.com (3rd row, right)
51: jamespharaon/istockphoto.com (San Jacinto Monument), SAKhanPhotography/istockphoto.com (Burj Khalifa), brilliantboy/istockphoto.com (Empire State Building), rcp/istockphoto.com (Washington Monument), Andrew_Howe/istockphoto.com (Statue of Liberty), Mooneydriver/istockphoto.com (space shuttle), hikesterson/istockphoto.com (home)
54: Apple Inc.
56: jeffstrauss/istockphoto.com
58: tap10/istockphoto.com (sunburned man)
60–61: Marilyn Nieves/istockphoto.com
62: PaaschPhotography/istockphoto.com
73: eurobanks/istockphoto.com (beer can)
74: Henrik_L/istockphoto.com (mosquito)
75: hangxu/istockphoto.com (boy crying), bluejayphoto/istockphoto.com (horse), mediaphotos/istockphoto.com (man), keithferrisphoto/istockphoto.com (couple)
78: GlobalP/istockphoto.com (skunk), kazina/istockphoto.com (turtles)
79: supermimicry/istockphoto.com (ants on fries)
80: LivingImages/istockphoto.com (cowboy), Yasin Emir Akbas/istockphoto.com (baby)
82: RobLopshire/istockphoto.com
84: George Manga/istockphoto.com
85: piovesempre/istockphoto.com (man), aryos/istockphoto.com (sun), RugliG/istockphoto.com (dirt), Clint Spencer/istockphoto.com (storm)
86: LUNAMARINA/istockphoto.com (traffic)
87: ferrantraite/istockphoto.com (two girls), Steve Debenport/istockphoto.com (girl)
92: David Hughes/istockphoto.com
94: steele2123/istockphoto.com (redneck), FlairImages/istockphoto.com (socialite), JMichl/istockphoto.com (dance hall angel), IPGGutenbergUKLtd/istockphoto.com (gun enthusiast)
95: ShannonCA/istockphoto.com (cowboy), FilippoBacci/istockphoto.com (hippie), Andrew Rich/istockphoto.com (cowgirl), g-stockstudio/istockphoto.com (hipster)
96 (cowgirl), 118 (father): DRB Images, LLC/istockphoto.com
96: Robert Ingelhart/istockphoto.com (cowboy), 4x6/istockphoto.com (musicians)
98: josepponsa/istockphoto.com
99: Pamela Moore/istockphoto.com (man)
112: zrfphoto/istockphoto.com
115: AnthiaCumming/istockphoto.com (football), andresr/istockphoto.com (fans), Jason Lugo/istockphoto.com (helmet)
118: Devonyu/istockphoto.com (whistle), XiXinXing/istockphoto.com (football player), Suljo/istockphoto.com (trumpet), DRB Images, LLC/istockphoto.com (man), Brian McEntire/istockphoto.com (cheerleader), DNY59/istockphoto.com (megaphone)
120: sihuo0860371/istockphoto.com (pickup), homeworks255/istockphoto.com (car), epantha/istockphoto.com (police car), kickstand/istockphoto.com (bus), PKM1/istockphoto.com (box truck)
121: lissart/istockphoto.com (band), blackred/istockphoto.com (quarter)
124: FernandoAH/istockphoto.com
126: NicholasBPhotography/istockphoto.com (corndog), studiocasper/istockphoto.com (beer), sumnersgraphicsinc/istockphoto.com (clowns)
127: earleliason/istockphoto.com (Ferris wheel)
138: russellart/istockphoto.com (pickle)
139: rimglow/istockphoto.com (salsa), marilyna/istockphoto.com (chips), arnet117/istockphoto.com (fruit cup)
143, 152 (veggies & shrimp): Lauri Patterson/istockphoto.com
144: HHLtDave5/istockphoto.com
145: apple2499/istockphoto.com
152 (hot dogs), 194 (girl with mittens): tacojim/istockphoto.com
152: dial-a-view/istockphoto.com (hamburgers), jcphoto/istockphoto.com (chicken), aassemany/istockphoto.com (corn), andhal/istockphoto.com (cow)
166: CSA-Printstock/istockphoto.com
192: stevecoleimages/istockphoto.com
194: djumandji/istockphoto.com (car fire)
195: Sam Camp/istockphoto.com (bison), motimeiri/istockphoto.com (skates)
196: 33ft/istockphoto.com
Back cover: baona/istockphoto.com (Kevin), Juanmonino/istockphoto.com (Eric), furtaev/istockphoto.com (Randy), DRB Images, LLC/istockphoto.com (Kim), beetle8/istockphoto.com (Dean), PacoRomero/istockphoto.com (Brian), bluejayphoto/istockphoto.com (Stu), Mr.Nikon/Shutterstock.com (Bob), Wavebreakmedia/istockphoto.com (Dorothy), limalo58/istockphoto.com (Braden), DRB Images, LLC/istockphoto.com (Stacey)